Anger Management

A Step-by-Step Guide to Take Control of Your Emotions in Every Situation and Grow Your Self-Help

By: Adam Goleman

Disclaimer Notice.

Please note the information contained within this document is for educational and entertainment purposes only. This book not intended to be a substitute for medical advice. Please consult your health care provider for medical advice and treatment.

Table of Content

Chapter 4: Don't Fall into Provocations

Chapter 5: Anger Management Advice

Chapter 6: Anger Management and Emotional Intelligence

Chapter 7: Mental Disorder, the Origin of Problems

Chapter 8: How to Increase your Self-Awareness

Chapter 9: Mindfulness, Use Mindfulness Techniques when you are Angry

Chapter 10: Cognitive Behavioral Therapy

Chapter 11: Meditation Techniques

Conclusion

Introduction

Anger is a strong feeling of annoyance, displeasure, or hostility towards someone or something. Anger usually occurs as a natural response to feeling attacked, frustrated, or even being humiliated. It is human nature to get angry. The fury, therefore, is not a bad feeling per se because, at times, it can prove to be very useful. How is this even possible? Anger can open one's mind and help them identify their problems which could drive one to get motivated to make a change and help in molding their lives.

When is anger a problem? Anger, as we have just seen, is normal in life. The problem only comes in when one cannot manage their anger, and it causes harm to people around them or even themselves. How does one notice when their anger is becoming harmful? When one starts expressing anger through unhelpful or destructive behavior, or even when one's mental and physical health starts deteriorating. That's when one knows that the situation is getting out of hand. It is the way a person behaves that determines whether or not they have problems with their anger. If the way they act affects their life or relationships, then there is a problem, and they should think about getting some support or treatment.

What is unhelpful angry behavior? Anger may be familiar to everyone, but people usually express their rage in entirely different ways. How one behaves when they are angry depends on how much control they have over their feelings. People who have less control over their emotions tend to have some unhelpful angry behaviors. These are behaviors that cause damage to themselves or even damage to people or things around them. They include:

Noticeable aggression and viciousness

This is where one aims his or her anger towards individuals or things nearby them. Some of the actions here may consist of yelling at people, being aggressive to people, banging doors, hitting or tossing things, or being orally abusive. These kinds of actions can be very worrisome and unsafe for people around, particularly children. They can cause spartan consequences similar to the loss of a career or even hurting a precious one or just essentially anyone around.

Inward aggression

This is where one directs their anger towards themselves. Some of the behaviors here may include telling oneself that they hate themselves, denying themselves, or even cutting themselves off the world.

Non-violent or passive aggression

In this case, one does not direct their anger anywhere; rather they stick with the feeling in them. Some of the behaviors here may include ignoring people, refusing to speak to people, refusing to do tasks, or even deliberately doing chores poorly or late. These types of behaviors are usually the worst ways to approach such situations. They may seem less destructive and harmful, but they do not relieve one of the heavy burdens that are causing them to be angry.

Preparation

Weigh your options - In life, many things may be out of one's control. These things vary from the weather, the past, other people, intrusive thoughts, physical sensations, and one's own emotions. Despite all these, the power to choose is always disposable to any human. Even though one might not be able to control the weather, one can decide whether or not to wear heavy clothing. One can also choose how to respond to other people. The first step, therefore, in dealing with anger is to recognize a choice.

Thank you for having this book.

Chapter 1: Understand the signs of your anger

Role of Anger

Getting angry usually relays an important message meant for good, but others may feel offended. Often, we get angry in an effort to be heard only to destroy relationships in the process. In intelligent communication, any form of aggression corrodes your true intent.

Communicating with passive aggression is worse as opposed to popular belief. Passive aggression may seem innocent from your words, but they are vicious. Most people opt for passive aggression, but it breaks connections. Therefore, you should consider a better strategy for a better understanding of people. Lately, people are taking to Twitter more and more for those indirect jabs.

Immediate Anger Expression Is Exceptional

Often, we find ourselves mad but can't remember how those feelings started. That is why it is advisable to express your feelings as they come; it helps the negativity go away faster. Extinguish the fire immediately you see smoke; waiting for the inferno doesn't do you any good. Same for your feelings—handle them as they emerge.

Reasons for You to Express Emotions Immediately

They become more intense when you wait. Contemplating your emotions magnifies their intensity. Getting rid of these emotions immediately saves you from more stress. It's easier to handle things before they blow up. People give advice on waiting when you're angry so that you don't regret it later. You regret actions and not feelings. Never be afraid to express what you feel.

There is a better understanding. Sharing your feelings immediately removes ambiguity over what made you mad or who did what. It just happened. Bottling up your emotions finds you being set off by minor issues. Confusion over the source of the sudden emotions only creates new conflict.

It's an opportunity for clarification in case of a misunderstanding. Most times, being angry with someone emanates from a misunderstanding. You may have interpreted them the wrong way. A simple explanation over the issue clears out the air.

It's unlikely to be fixed unless something is said. The receiving party and everyone else around you do not mind readers. They could never know how you feel unless you tell them. They may be part of the solution; there is no point in holding back.

You don't have to fake it. It's draining to hide your emotions with your actions. Being true to yourself is important for both your emotional health and a healthy state of mind.

You don't have to bottle your emotions. Avoiding your emotions doesn't make them disappear. On the contrary, stuffed-up emotions have been linked to several physiological ailments. They include depression, asthma, anger, high blood pressure, and infections.

You are more comfortable with your feelings. When you are aware of your emotions and are able to express them, you become comfortable enough to obtain information crucial in decision making.

Your feelings change. The best way to get rid of negative emotions is to get over them. You only get over them by recognizing them and expressing them in a healthy way. Psychologists agree that talking your heart out completely although angry manifests positive feelings. I mean you always feel better if you talk to a friend.

You create stronger bonds. People avoid their emotions in fear of being rejected. Ironically, being honest and vulnerable provide a strong base for good relationships. You know the other person better with them expressing themselves. You also get to know how your actions affect the other.

Your family and friends start doing the same. People close to you follow your lead if you express your feelings freely. With the same benefits, they become emotionally healthier. This makes you closer to them.

Chapter 2: How anger affects relationships

Expressing Your Anger While Conserving Relationships

In the event you are angry, neither passive aggression nor the extreme direct approach is advised. They destroy your relationships. Instead, follow the guides below:

Become self-aware

Never be too quick to express your frustration. Instead, take a minute for cooler heads to prevail. When our emotions are running high, we are never thinking straight. Be conscious of what's really going on for more effective communication. Take a walk, exercise, meditate or pray for you to regain your composure for a better perspective on the whole situation.

Understand your emotions

Often, we confuse hurt and sadness with anger, which might be easier to express. Frustration could well be pain, sorrow, or rejection. Pinpoint on the real emotion you feel in order to communicate with honesty, hence more effectively.

Be on the lookout for misplaced blame

Always find the root of your anger. You may just be hungry, going through stuff, exhausted, or lacking sleep. Don't dish it out to the next innocent person that crosses your path. Sometimes, it's easier to assign blame as we find it taxing than to think of the real reason behind our frustrations. However, it only drives people we care about away. Nothing is resolved until the real burning issue is tackled.

Be curious

Curiosity helps us see the bigger picture. In our frustrations, we forget there is the other person's perspective only thinking of yourself. Try moving away from being self-centered and ask why the other person made you mad. It couldn't have been intentional. Confronting them doesn't get you real reasons. Care a little as they might be going through something you can help. Try understanding that the other person doesn't aim to hurt you on purpose. You may even get over your anger so easily with a little understanding.

Be compassionate

Don't be quick to assume the worst of people. Try to understand what they're going through along with their point of view. Always show respect for people's feelings, and understand why they act in a certain way. This opens up for effective communication. With compassion and empathy, your relationships get deeper. Aggressive communication makes people angry and defensive in return. Giving people an opportunity to share their perspective makes them respect yours even more.

Communicate with skill

In effective communication, skills like compassion, curiosity, and compromise go a long way. Don't just stop at sharing your feelings, or you'll be self-centered. Go a step further and ask the other party to share it with you. Show interest and be ready to compromise. Never accuse someone without their side of the story.

How to Deal with Passive-Aggressive People

Call them out

Never give anyone a pass for showing aggression in any way. You might as well ask how they meant with their words. People don't expect to be called out when they are passive-aggressive. Ask more questions to get to the root of what bothers them. A grown-up conversation over how they feel would be one way to show them another way.

Ignore them

Even though the other party is trying to get the point across, you shouldn't be drawn into their hostile attitude. Soon as you engage, you enter the same state of mind, which is unhealthy. You live happier by letting such situations go.

Show forgiveness and a little compassion

Tension and frustration cause one to show aggression either directly or passively. Don't be so hard on such a person; they are already getting it bad. Just set boundaries for your own sake, but forgive them and wish them good vibes.

Invite them to share their own feelings and perspective

Show the other party that there is a better way of handling your aggression. Leading by example works best. When you express your negative emotions, ask them to do the same. Soon they move away from passive-aggressive tactics that only worsen their situations.

In conclusion, it's okay to be mad and frustrated

The important matter is to express it in a healthy way. Proper expression of your negative emotions can leave you feeling better. Funny enough, it might as well be a misunderstanding needing clarification. It's not healthy to be playing okay but you're not. Bottled emotions can make you sick emotionally and physically, too. You see the benefits as soon as you learn to communicate emotions effectively.

While it is important to express your feelings as they emerge, bear in mind you have relationships to conserve. It's not worth it losing friends because you got mad. Apply communication skills. Don't be self-centered.

Inquire and be ready to listen and understand the other person's perspective. As you realize, communicating truly has advantages; your family and friends follow suit and reap the same benefits. It is therefore important to notice people with aggressive communication and show them a better way, or just avoid their interactions.

Chapter 3: "How to" Transforming the energy of anger

Run the Stress Off

Running is a great way of combating stress. It is one of the easiest and beneficial physical exercises anyone can engage in.

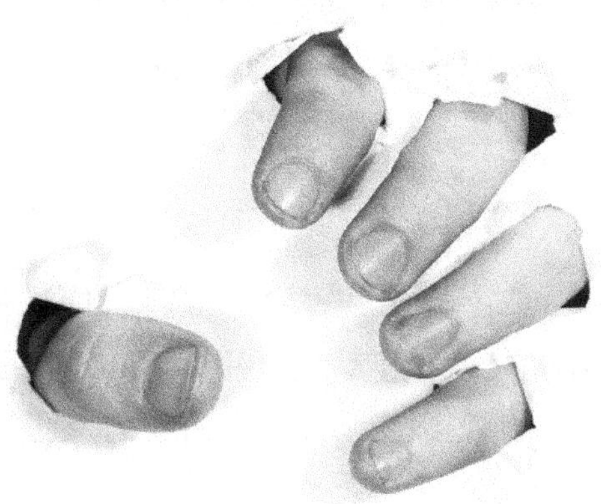

If you are feeling beat down by the rigors of life, take a run down your street or get to the nearest field and run a few laps. There are several benefits that you will experience if you run regularly:

- Running is an aerobic exercise that increases the heart rate and makes you sweat, hence activating chemicals known as endorphins in the body which are responsible for making us feel good, leaving your brain elated and making you happy.
- You will shed calories which will help with lowering your blood pressure and keeping your arteries in good shape.
- Running slows the aging process and reduces bone and muscle loss by building strength and flexibility. It keeps you active and improves your overall health.
- When running, you have all the time to yourself which allows you to process your thoughts. You may use the time to aid you with sorting out some issues that you may be facing or to think through a problem.
- Researchers have found out that people who are regular runners lead a happier, more stress-free life and are generally fitter than those who do not. Your concentration and alertness are also enhanced.

Now, put on those running shoes and hit the road for a healthier, happier, and stress-free life. Running can be done almost anywhere you go, you do not have to worry about where to perform this exercise. It is recommended that you drink a lot of water if you are a runner; drink at least a liter of water an hour to two hours before your run. This helps with hydration of the body and you are unlikely to suffer dehydration. You will not regret your decision as the benefits that will accrue to you are many.

Take a Hike

Hiking is a relaxing walk through a natural surrounding usually at a nature trail, a park, or a forest. Much like running, hiking is a great exercise for stress relief though less vigorous. Hiking combines the benefits of an effective aerobic exercise, natural serene surrounding, and the chance and time to relax and think freely. The following are ways by which hiking helps the body to deal with stress:

Brain exercising

A hike will afford you the silence and time to think profoundly about things that are important to you. Aerobic exercise coupled with deep thinking will effectively enhance the body's stress management capabilities.

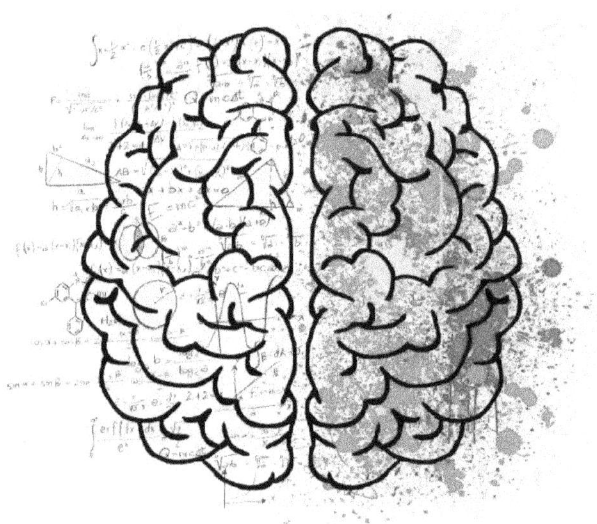

Mental relaxation

Hiking provides the time and opportunity for mind relaxation by getting you up close to nature. Nature has been proven as a catalyst for mental relaxation by giving you the experience and wonders of natural surroundings.

Energizing the Body

Hiking, being an aerobic exercise, invigorates the body and helps with the regulation of stress chemicals. People who hike regularly have higher levels of feel-good hormones like endorphins which reduce stress considerably.

Emotional wellbeing

When you are stressed, you are a prisoner of negative emotions like sadness, anger, nervousness, etc. Hiking will activate positive energy in your body which will, in turn, boost your emotions to make you feel better and happier.

Spiritual nourishment

Being in a natural environment with the wonderful serenity offers the body a chance to get spiritually fulfilled. Your nerves will be calmed and you will get the opportunity for mental clarity and relaxation that you would normally not have every day. Hiking is a great exercise for anger and stress relief and you ought to prepare in advance before you go on a hike. Pack a first aid kit, drinking water, and a phone in case you may be confronted with an accident.

Come on, why don't you start hiking for a change? It may just be the answer to dealing with the stress you have been under lately. So, book an appointment with nature for exercise, mental and spiritual fulfillment, and say goodbye to stress and anger.

Pedal the Stress Away

Do you remember how happy you were riding your bicycle when you were young? I remember my experience and I could give anything to feel the same way again. Exciting, happy, and a sense of unbridled freedom. It was just a great time without a care in the world. Well, you do not have to look back to your childhood with such nostalgia because you can readily bring back those feel-good moments you had on your bicycle to the present to replace all the anger and worries you are facing now!

Don't you want to?

Cycling is another form of aerobic exercise that is great for stress relief, fitness, and general well-being. When you are overwhelmed by life's pressures, simply hop on a bike and start pedaling for stress relief. Being on the bike will take your mind off the problems that are bothering you. Pump some feel-good chemicals into your bloodstream. Pace your heart to leave you feeling refreshed and emotionally elated.

You can cycle after work, on weekends, or your day off or even to work and while doing this, employ the meditative technique of mantra by chanting a positive phrase or word to the rhythm of your pedaling. I assure you that you will be surprised at how fast your mind will be cleared off the negativity and stress that you are facing.

Cycling is not an expensive endeavor; just buy a bicycle and you may start. It is not vigorous if done for leisure or exercise and can be taken up by people of all ages. Cycling will keep you fit and work out your heart for better health and emotional balance. It helps with the management of chronic conditions like diabetes, cardiovascular problems, and high blood pressure. The healthier and better you feel, the less likely you are to be stressed. Get on your bike and enjoy the stress-relieving benefits you have been missing.

Reading for Stress Relief

Reading is cathartic and is a great reliever of stress for people who are facing everyday pressures and adversity by relaxing the brain and managing the thought process. When you read, your mind travels away from the pressures you are facing. You sink into the story where you will find yourself in faraway worlds. In the duration of your reading, you shall be transported away from your troubles and this helps in balancing your emotional wellbeing.

Reading is a great mental exercise that stimulates brain activity thereby improving mental concentration and alertness. Stress fighting chemicals that give you a happy feeling are released into the brain. An active mind is strong and more likely to cope with daily pressures. You will also fight stress from the motivation and hope you derive from reading biographies and motivational books. Books and other literature are sources of information that enables you to learn more and aid in problem solving.

A book will divert your thoughts from the lingering problems or worries that are stressing you out. Set aside a few hours in your day to read and you will experience how fulfilling it can be in your efforts at dealing with stress.

When you clear your mind of negativity even for a few hours, you will make huge strides in mental relaxation. With a relaxed mind, you should be able to be more creative and relaxed enabling you to cope with stress. An active mind also slows down the aging process leaving you feeling younger physically and mentally. A strong healthy body is less prone to stress.

If the last time you read was for an exam or for a school assignment, make a hot cup of tea, make yourself comfortable on your favorite seat, and immerse yourself into a book. The benefits for your life and health are great, you need to try it. Get literature that appeals to you, a book, magazine, or newspaper and make it a habit to read regularly for a less-stress life every day.

Be a Positive Thinker

Have you heard of positive thinking? Well, the world works in a very simple way in that whatever you think is what will be manifested in your life. You attract what you think! It may seem simplistic or difficult to accept but take the time to mull it over and you realize that it is true. If you want to get that new job you applied to or want to get promoted, it begins by you want it, then believing that you can get it without having a shred of doubt.

Self-belief is a powerful stress reliever. To always be positive and to be ever optimistic. The power of positive thinking is incredible. If you look forward to good things, you will have a happier, less stressful life. Positive thinking is a state where you look forward to favorable outcomes in whatever you do. Positive thinking, therefore, involves actively training your mind to have creative thoughts that transform energy into reality.

Avoid dwelling on your failures and concentrate on the successes; use the disappointments as lessons for the future. Studies show that positive thinking leads to a longer and healthier life since you are less prone to stress. You become a positive thinker by identifying the negative aspects of your thinking and avoid them while constantly evaluating your thoughts to make sure you stay on the positive.

Do not be too hard on yourself. Allow yourself joyous moments and take time to have fun. Surround yourself with like-minded people who will help you build the habit of positive thinking. When you are optimistic, you become less critical and are instead more creative and hopeful. An optimistic mindset is able to deal with stress at work more easily and constructively. Positive thinking is a powerful tool for fighting stress and anger. Try it and you are sure of great benefits and happy relaxed life.

Time Management

If you are always late and short of time, then you are most likely leading a stressed and anxious life. There is nothing as stressful as the struggle to always meet a deadline or catch up with something you forgot about. Using the little time we have properly will help you cope with stress. Time management involves methods aimed at using time efficiently to perform all the tasks we have within a given time and involves prioritizing, scheduling, and organizing.

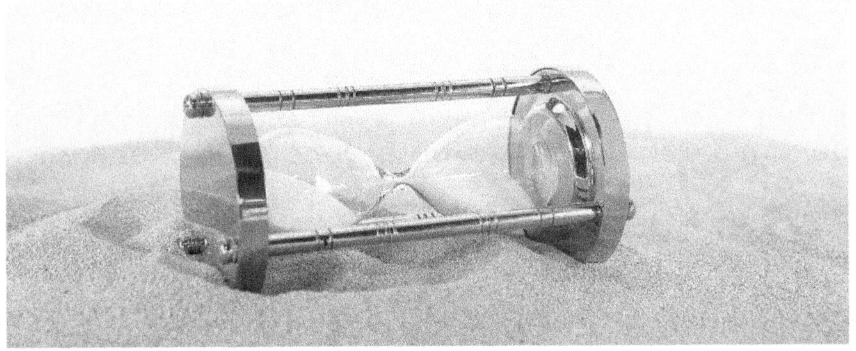

You must assess the tasks on your plate and put them in order of importance and urgency to avoid confusion, conflicts, and unnecessary time pressures. Plan things in advance to avoid last-minute scrambling in an effort to get something that skipped your mind done. Good time management makes you a more productive person. You will do more within a short time thus gaining more control of your life.

Create a schedule and stick to it. You will have enough free time to engage in fun things that you have been missing. You will have time to go to the movies, play a game, or any other fun activity which serves to boost health and wellbeing. Good time management means that you have enough time for work, family, and friends. These moments with loved ones are the most fulfilling and stress relieving.

It does not take much to be a good time manager. All you need is to start and commit to it. Well managed time leads to a more comfortable and happy life. Benefits of time management for a less stressful life are:

- ➢ Doing more with less time.
- ➢ Getting more free time which allows time to relax.
- ➢ Stress is reduced since you do not worry about pending deadlines etc.

- ➢ Higher productivity since you are fresh mentally, physically and highly motivated.
- ➢ Time management is good because you will be happier, more successful, more productive, and live a fuller and stress-free life. Why don't you start managing your time better and enjoy the benefits?

Get Enough Sleep

Are you sleeping enough? Lack of adequate sleep is a big contributor to the incidences of stress and anger. Getting sufficient sleep is essential in your effort to deal with stress. During sleep, your body gets the chance to rest, to heal, and to be rejuvenated. When you do not get enough sleep, you are left susceptible to stress and other health problems because you are emotionally imbalanced.

Therefore, it is imperative to have a sleeping schedule and follow it so that you condition your body into a routine for sufficient rest. In fact, sleep deficiency is a great source of stress and anger since you are tired, irritable, and have weakened creativity. Between work and your personal affairs, you probably end up not getting enough sleep. It is recommended that you sleep for at least six hours for optimal rest. However, many of us do not meet this target as studies show that most of us sleep for as little as two hours and a maximum of four hours in a 24-hour cycle!

We do not get sufficient sleep because of our poor bedtime habits that end up interfering with our sleep. To sleep better and longer, try the following:

- ➢ Set a sleeping schedule. You will sleep better if your bedtime is predictable. Your body will adapt and you will rest more.

- ➢ Do not indulge in a heavy meal during dinner. Have a light meal at least two hours before you retire to bed.

- ➢ Physical exercise is a great sleep inducer. Work out three to four hours before you sleep.

- ➢ Do not take caffeinated drinks close to your bedtime. Your last caffeine drink should be averagely six hours or more before you lay down.

- ➢ Keep away from alcohol four to six hours before your bedtime. It will disrupt your sleep.

- ➢ Sleep well for emotional balance. You will wake up refreshed, well-rested, and energized. When your body has this balance, it can easily manage or ward off stress.

Listening To Soothing Music

Music is very relaxing and has the ability to change moods positively by acting on our minds to avert stress. It acts quickly, is available, and will relieve you of stress and anger. The calming effect of music has a distinctive relationship to our emotions and is an effective way to cope with stress. Slow classical music is extremely peaceful and has a positive effect on our bodies and minds. This kind of music has its advantages. It slows the heart and pulse rates, reduces the production of stress hormones and blood pressure.

Music engrosses our thoughts to distract us from whatever worries may be lingering in our minds. Most times, when you are stressed and anxious, your mind tends to wander off causing you to think of the things that cause you more anger. However, music acts as a cushion and helps your mind to relax and better concentrate.

For years, music has been proven to treat ailments and restore coherence and balance between your body and mind. Furthermore, research has it that music is therapeutic in the following ways:

- Some music compositions can help disabled people by boosting harmonization and communication and improve their life.

- The use of headphones when listening to music can lessen anger and stress especially when one is about to go for surgery and after the surgery.

- During extreme pain or post-surgery, music has been known to ease and numb the pain.

- Music is also known to alleviate depression and enhance self-esteem in older people.

- Soothing music has been proven to improve mood and reduce burnout.

- Music is therapeutic especially for cancer patients as it improves the quality of life and reduces emotional trauma.

- Music is food for the soul. The next time you are facing adversity or are feeling down from mental fatigue or some other worries, turn on your favorite music. Enjoy the relaxing and positive vibes that will be provided by the music.

Share your Problems by Talking to Someone

A problem shared is a problem solved or half solved. How insightful this is. Sharing our problems is therapeutic and a quick fix to stress. Putting a lid on your suffering and keeping it to yourself is an emotional burden and is very unhealthy. Many of us are fiercely independent and would want to solve our problems on our own. However, there is a point where you are better off talking to someone about what you are going through.

Pent up emotions and suffering will turn you into a very stressed and imbalanced person. Reach out to someone you trust, a friend or relative, for a listening ear and realize the great positive impact it will have on you. Talking to someone has the following benefits:

- ➢ Sharing your problems will help you get rid of bad emotions like worries, anger, etc. You will feel better after since you will have let go of the emotional burden.
- ➢ Your pain is reduced since you will have someone sharing your problem and empathizing with you.

- ➢ Solutions to your problems are easier to come by, as you will be readily advised by the listener.
- ➢ By sharing, you lead a healthier life since you negate the effects of emotional distress caused by pent up emotional turmoil.
- ➢ You will simply feel better and happier at having talked about whatever is bothering you.

By sharing, we get the load off our chests leaving us emotionally boosted, relaxed, and stronger. It also prevents the situation from deteriorating to a much deeper problem like depression or emotional breakdown. With a relaxed and more stable mental state, you have the clarity and strength to handle your problem, and will easily embark on problem solving for a stress-free life.

From now on, if you find yourself in a tight place emotionally and are feeling stressed, seek someone you can share your problem with and enjoy the quick stress relief that comes with it.

You Should Laugh More

The benefits of laughter in coping with stress and for a healthier life are numerous. It is proven that humor is a powerful tool for stress relief. Try and laugh and be cheerful despite the tough times. Laughter has a way of rubbing off on others, so if you are happy, those around you will follow and you will be surrounded by happiness. A happy life is a stress-free life.

Laughter enhances oxygen intake and stimulates the functioning of body organs like the heart, brain, and lungs. Your heart rate is also improved for better blood flow and cardiovascular wellbeing. By laughing your way through life, you benefit from muscle relaxation and tension relief. Your immunity will be enhanced through the release of stress-fighting chemicals in the body. All the pain you are suffering emotionally and even physically is reduced by laughter which triggers the production of the body's natural pain-killing hormones.

A happy person is a magnet, attracting people for improved social life and emotional state. So, when you are downcast, just smile through it; you will feel better. In any case, the difficulties will soon pass and with a positive and happy approach, you will survive it.

Laughter subdues toxic stress attracting thoughts, help you forget your worries, and enables you to concentrate and work on the tasks at hand. Be happy and grateful for the good things that you have been blessed with. Think about them when you are stressed. Laugh and smile as you recollect and be assured of a stress-free life.

A good sense of humor is not a panacea but it is sure to improve your outlook at life, your health, and your social standing. A good laugh will do you a lot of good smiles and laugh more; laughter is indeed the best medicine.

Eat Healthy Foods

Food is the fuel and the source of nourishment for the body; an integral part of our general wellbeing and good health. It is important that we eat the right foods and eat well for us to stay healthy. A healthy body is able to fend off the side effects of stress with ease.

Food and stress are uniquely interwoven. When faced with adversity, some people have a sudden craving for food while others will lose their appetite. It is, therefore, necessary that we know the right foods to eat, especially when we are under some sort of stress. When we encounter stress, we crave comfort foods such as fats and sugars. These foods are not healthy and cause harm to us and will cause us more stress. To stay healthy and manage stress, we have to avoid:

> Consumption of a lot of fast foods because they are unhealthy and more expensive than cooking for yourself, in the long run.

> Skipping meals because it is a catalyst for stress. If you miss meals, you are likely to be fatigued and less nourished thus susceptible to stress.

> Too much caffeinated drinks which interfere with your sleep and deny you adequate rest.

> Eating the wrong food types. Eat a balanced diet and resist the temptation of eating too much of foods rich in fats and sugars. These foods only lead to weight gain and cardiovascular problems.

A poor diet will leave you with problems of hormonal imbalance and weight problems – either loss or too much gain. You will develop a weak immune system and are likely to be susceptible to illnesses. Unhealthy eating will also lead to an imbalance of the blood sugar which may lead to diabetes. Stress makes your body burn nutrients you consume much faster than normal that is why you should be on a healthy diet. It is wise that you replenish these nutrients to help cope with stress.

Balancing Between Your Life and Work

Continually working without getting a break does not only make you less productive but you easily get bored with your work. You will also become boring to your colleagues. You need to have some time away from your job to have fun and engage in things that excite you and pump your blood. Most adults who are stressed can trace the source to their work because we spend a lot of time on the job. It is, therefore, important to balance the time we spend working and time for ourselves for a healthier lifestyle.

Work-life balance is about dividing your time effectively and adequately between work and your private life. If you let work consume most of your time and neglect or shortchange your personal needs, you will end up stressed. When your personal life is in order, you are less likely to be stressed since you will worry less. Your mind will not be stretched from being divided between what you need to do at work and the personal matters awaiting your attention.

Spend time with family and friends. It is relaxing and healthy for you. When was the last time you went cycling or shopping with your children? These mundane activities are the foundation of a well-balanced healthy life devoid of stress. If your private life brings you happiness, you will able to face pressures that come your way. After spending time with your loved ones, you need to set aside personal time for things that are self-gratifying. Go for a massage or run a few laps at the neighborhood field, volunteer your services for a worthy cause, etc. Such acts are great for boosting your emotional wellbeing.

If you embrace a healthy work-life balance, you will reap the many benefits. Personal nourishment and care are important for overall health. Balance your private and professional life for a stress-free healthy life where you are happier and revitalized.

Write, Pick Up Your Pen and Paper

Another technique of dealing with stress is writing. It is especially encouraged when one is so stressed or depressed. Putting down your experience, feelings, and thoughts in a journal is very therapeutic for recovery and for defeating stress. Writing works by clarifying your mind and thoughts and it is a form of therapy in the sense that it compels you to recall events and thoughts of the day on paper to give you a better avenue to analyze and understand what happened. It is also meditative. It slows down your heart as you focus on your writing to stream out your thoughts to paper.

Writing sharpens and stimulates brain functioning and activity to improve your mental acuity and concentration as well as improving your vocabulary. You are, therefore, better equipped to handle stressful situations. When you write regularly, the stress triggers in your head are disrupted allowing you to better relax and sleep better. You get up well-rested and energized. Writing also fights anger by removing the thoughts from your mind to the writing pad, essentially offering you a platform to vent it out.

When you write down your worries and problems it is easier to solve them. Writing allows you to identify what the problem is, think it through overtime, and most likely, come up with a great unrushed solution and avert the stress that you may have. Having a to-do list or schedule helps you focus and get organized. You are able to plan in advance to avoid last-minute rushes or procrastination that will only serve to make your life stressful.

Writing will boost your immune system. By slowing your breathing, you are able to breathe in more oxygen to better nourish the brain and blood leading to faster healing and an enhanced ability to fight pathogens. Better breathing also strengthens the lungs, which has a positive effect in fighting respiratory conditions like asthma. To reap the benefits of writing for better health and stress relief, it does not matter what you write, the main thing is to be able to jot down your thoughts and review them. You do not have to be a John Grisham! Write down what is on your mind because the healing power lies in you letting out the negative thoughts that are weighing on your mind.

Chapter 4: Don't Fall into Provocations

Anger Triggers

Individuals that suffer from anger are not affected by the indications which may be present in situations that they encounter socially. Whenever they feel confident about the people they are interacting with who may include their peers, work colleagues, their sisters/brothers, the inner circle of friends, their family members including extended, chances are there will be a failure to exhibit any manifestation of anger in any way. They are also confident while speaking to a large audience concerning a topic they are well conversant with.

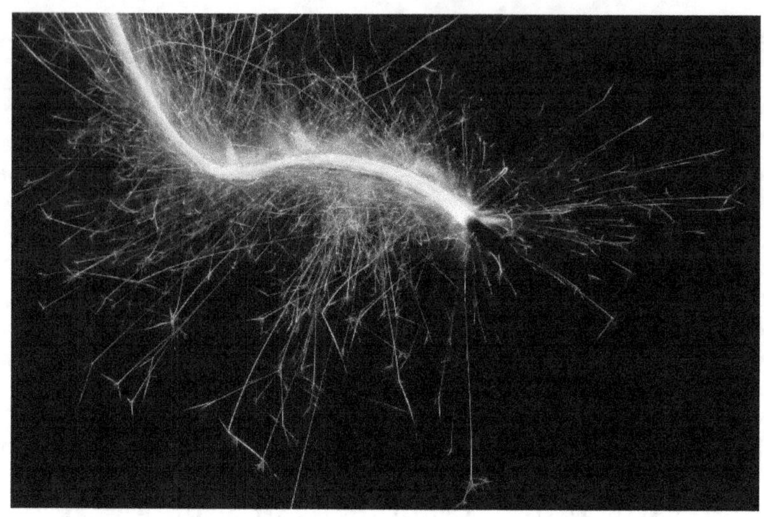

However, several circumstances can lead to agony and anger. Although, the anger expressed may not seem to bother or threaten a large group of people. A number of the commonly known and studied motivators for anger patients are:

- ➤ Abuse in terms of language
- ➤ Disrespect
- ➤ Invasion of personal space
- ➤ Injustice
- ➤ Shaming
- ➤ Lies
- ➤ Threats, mostly physically
- ➤ Being teased or kidded.

People with anger disorder, most of the time, conclude that being made fun of is something personal. They do this by:

> Feeling uneasy when someone is looking at them while they perform a task they are not familiar with
> Lack of self-control
> Relationship wrangles

A lot of people with an anger problem have more than three circumstances that make them react in an anxious and overwhelming manner. They usually do their best to get away from such causes as much as possible. Although there may be other instances that these circumstances occur, the signals of anger may be less extreme but the end results end up making life hard and strenuous.

Tackling an Anger Problem

When anger is not diagnosed and consequently not treated, it is very devastating and eventually affects how one functions daily. After an individual realizes they have an anger problem, they may not have the strength to seek help. They keep away from therapists, making sure not to interact with them in any way. Truth be told, treatment for anger problems is highly effective and the results achieved in a short or long time are commendable.

Though doctor prescribes medicine to curb depression and anger, going through psychotherapy is highly recommended. Treatment that helps with cognition and behavior (CBT) is mostly recommended by doctors who have patients with an anger disorder. These treatments are offered on an outpatient basis. Nonetheless, individuals who have had anger struggles over the years benefit greatly when they are admitted so that they can concentrate on recovering.

Under the programs are residential, CBT, and other services that are essential. They are also offered but in an atmosphere that centers solely on the patient. In these programs, they may interact with their peers who are facing a similar challenge and they get to know ways of overcoming the challenges they have.

Although anger is not an easy experience, by using specialists and medication, it's controllable. Anger can frustrate and fascinate when the individual experiences it, they might seek to know, "What lead to anger? Why do I have to cope with this?" Curiosity can occur even when you, as an individual, is not a victim. You may have a close friend or family member having an anger problem or you get to explore deeper on the deeper issues concerning. No matter the reasons, getting to know the causes is important. These will enable you to be in a better position to empathize with the millions of people who cope with an anger disorder.

If you keep on giving yourself restrictions, and even in the process of tiring someone, then getting to know the causes is the first step.

The main causes of anger that are widely known are seven. They cause anger that is within. These are:

> Past encounters and environments as well as impacts associated with parenting style, trauma, and so on.
> Behaviors that are maladaptive and behaviors that have a negative effect.
> The temperament that is negatively affected by behavior and a style that not securely connected.
> Anger that is genetically passed down generations.
> A neurological disorder which is associated with overactivity in specific areas of the brain linked to anger
> The adverse effects of technology where individuals do not take time to converse face to face and they also do not have time for themselves.
> Physical causes such as being in situations and events that will make men and women be anxious, hence set in motion the characteristic which accompanies anger.

These factors influence each other in certain ways. Going through experience, being in an environment which is linked to interactions socially result in men and women developing bad beliefs and maladaptive behaviors. These beliefs and behaviors may cause and nurture interpersonal anger. The cognitive results then change brain construction and functioning.

Anger that is passed down genetically, through character and being attached, is more likely to result in anger disorder. When individuals panic socially, then a number of triggers are set off thereby opening them up to various anger signs. These include setting themselves apart and being agitated.

In order to familiarize ourselves with the above, let us go to the next topic.

Overcoming anger

Earlier on, I talked about the nature and frequency of anger. When you find yourself reserved and nervous in a diversity of social circumstances such as talking in front of a group of people, meeting new individuals, using communal closets or rest places, or even drinking in public, you may fear that certain individuals will realize your fear and get humiliated. This might show you that you're suffering from anger disorder. A lot of folks with this problem will decide to avoid circumstances where they forestall being nervous or they might take alcohol or else drugs to self-medicate before entering these circumstances. Personal anger is related to amplified risk for alcoholic drinks abuse, unhappiness, loneliness, abridged occupational, progression, and the augmented likelihood of hanging around single.

Cognitive behavioral counselors make great advances for a drug-free approach to dealing with these problems. Right now, there is considerable proof that Cognitive Behavior Therapy is an efficient treatment for anger. This particular remedy focuses on your behavior and what you are thinking about. So, let's take a closer take look at how this approach can help you overcome your social panic.

The particular behavioral problem for those with anger is the tendency to avoid anger-provoking situations. When the socially anxious individual anticipates heading to a celebration, he or she becomes quite anxious. However, when he chooses not to go, the anger immediately subsides. This reduction of panic with the decision to avoid the party, or to leave a party, strengthens avoidance or escape. This simple reward for avoidance confirms the concern of negative social examination even when the individual really does not experience humiliation. For example, if I feel stressed thinking of approaching someone and then I decide to avoid talking with him or her, my panic immediately subsides. This immediate decrease in anger dictates that for me to feel less anxious, I should just avoid interacting with other people.

A significant issue of CBT is to aid the person to practice imminent social situations and sojourn in them so as to know that nothing is really bad will perhaps transpire and that their anger will decrease. An individual also learns that he can do it and the simple willingness to confront his fears is empowering. You start realizing that you are not the sort of person who can actually try this kind of thing. The first step in helping people with anger is to identify the situations that they are avoiding. You can make a listing of the types of situations that you feel anxious in or avoid. For instance, one person realized that using a public toilet where he was worried that individuals would observe him, meeting people at a party, speaking up at a meeting, and talking to a woman for the first time were some of his anger triggers. What are the situations that provoke your anger? What are you likely to avoid? Make a listing.

Setting up a hierarchy of fear

For every situation, you can identify how the situation could be rated in terms of how much anger that you would experience. You can rate each anticipated response on a scale of 0 to 10 depending on the level of anger that you might expect. One would mean there is no anger while 10 would signify a panic attack. For instance, a young man with the fear of meeting people at a party experienced the following stages of fear, from the lowest to the highest. Thinking of going to the party rates at three, going to the party is at five, walking into the room ranked at six, seeing people in the room is also number six, deciding to begin a conversation rests at number eight, and talking with a stylish woman. It's important to write down your predictions so as to be able to find a way of discovering how nervous you really are as you go. Most of the time, folks realize that they're not as apprehensive as they expected they would appear.

Test your Expectations

We often fail to recall the fact that we deal healthier than we assumed it we would. This is an inordinate chance to examine your exact predictions. As I stated above, you can write down how worried you think you'll be for anything that you do. What's the level of the rage that you anticipate? How far will you stay anxious? Precisely, what is your prediction? This is how you can examine your disastrous fortune-telling. For example, a middle-aged man who was informally anxious foretold that he might have a level of rage at nine for the whole extent of speaking with a lady at a party. He projected that his brains would go blank and that he'd be so nervous that he would want to leave. As a result, he was very concerned when he started a conversation, but when he was into the conversation, his anger decreased to level three. He did not walk away and, in fact, he got the impression that the lady he was talking to actually adored him. As a result, be clear of what you're predicting so you can find out if you're antedating more than what actually occurs. Maintain a constant record of your expectations.

Determine your behaviors and eradicate them

A lot of people are anxious about irrational behaviors that they consider to led them to safety or more likely to embarrass themselves. These safety 'manners' consist of self-medicating with intoxicating drinks or drugs, making yourself very stiff, evading attention contact, holding a mug tightly so that folks will not realize your hands are trembling, wiping your hands so as people won't notice you are perspiring, rehearsing precise what accurately you'll say, and speaking very fast. The problem with defensive behaviors is that they're like the training tires on a bicycle and they allow you to believe the only way you can get over this knowledge is to use the exercise wheels.

Chapter 5: Anger Management Advice

The optimistic part of the handling 'behavioral and cognitive' side of anger has resulted in an extraordinary result. Evidence that is proven in a clinical and research methodology concludes that therapy offered comprehensively in a behavioral and cognitive way has a positive lasting effect on individuals.

Through being persistent and consistent, anger can be brought under control and eventually eradicated. Each and every individual can progress positively when given the right treatment. In several centers that deal with anger, behavioral and cognitive therapy is referred to as comprehensive, hence separating it from the concepts that cognitive therapy is simplistic and only uses a number of strategies.

A program that will have sufficiently solved anger difficulties should address all the scholarly methods, procedures, and important factors that give room for the mind to drastically revolutionize. The mind is continually learning. Illogical thoughts and standards can change, therefore, this needs a cognitive procedure. The perfect response should disclose the events they're used to.

Looking for Anger Solutions

Anger, together with other anger challenges, can be treated successfully. In line with looking for a solution, you should also visit a specialist. Consult a person who:

- knows this problem well

- Handle it through experience

Arm yourself with information as a customer by asking questions. One way to inform yourself is seeking to know whether the counselor perceives your self-consciousness which is caused by being looked at by others and them having an unpleasant opinion about you. Or are they not paying much attention to what you are saying and answering in the negative, suggesting you are fine. What you are feeling is an exaggeration.

Though the feeling of being looked at or judged increases our self-consciousness. If your therapist does not understand this, then he/she does not have the capability of helping you. Hence, keep in mind that the professional should always welcome your questions. A therapist should be kind and accommodative, enabling you to speak out what is bothering you freely. If they do not have these qualities in the foreground, then they are suitable.

Individuals who are on the way to recovery from anger and its effects need to be supported, encouraged, and be in a friendly atmosphere so as to enhance the healing process. An atmosphere that is calm helps in learning the habits that need to be acquired so as to tackle the various effects of anger in our lives and eventually anger itself. This has a ripple effect on every area of the individual.

There are words that a therapist should not use. Like, you should tackle your fears head-on and they will eventually disappear. Anyone who has undergone social panic has tried to tackle their fears and these statements are not helpful at all. It is imperative to get a therapist who will help you through the process of healing from anger adequately.

Although learning how to handle anger and eventually overcoming is not a one-off thing, it can be done in a consistent and systematic manner. When most people are tackling with anger problems, they may feel overwhelmed and may not be willing to go through the healing process. That is why a qualified therapist will encourage and lead the individual on the right path to healing.

The following are special aspects involved in anger management:

- A clear perception of the underlying issues.

- Being dedicated to following through the treatment which may seem repetitive

- Finding ways of practicing and exercising what you have learned so that these cognitive methods become habitual and automated

- Be part of a team. Here you can activate fully and slowly tackle the triggers and the various aspects of anger in your life.

For example, if you cannot gather the strength to stand before an audience and read out loudly, then there are ways that one can use to tackle your fear/situation. The therapist can also form groups where an individual's role play in various tasks, for example, an interview before a panel of judges to enable each individual to reach their intended goal.

Groups

Anger behavior treatment groups should not push or persuade individuals to engage in group activities if they are not interested. Each individual should be left to freely choose whether they want to participate or not. This does not mean the treatment they are undergoing is not working. Each individual has a variety of anger issues that should be handled in a different manner. For some groups, a session is not the way to go, so they should not be coerced into participating in any activity they do not want.

There should be motivation and positive undertakings in the group which will, in turn, enable the participants to reciprocate. When this is achieved, they are able to positively progress towards tackling what is ailing them socially. For all this to take place, the therapist must now what methods to use so as to achieve the desired results.

Nowadays, the treatment of behaviors and cognitive can handle the stress that is in the social sphere. This therapy does not dwell on the past by bringing it to the foreground. Rather, the day-to-day challenges are handled using various techniques that do away with thoughts on anger, including what we believe and feel.

Some individuals start worrying when they know they have attended an event. This may take place many days before the event. Then, they now worry about how they conducted themselves and what others thought about them. In general, there is no single reason why people suffer from anger disorder.

Having the same genes i.e. family members can be responsible. People from the same family who have suffered from a social phobia may pass on the genes to their kin. Inter-personal panic attacks usually start when an individual is at the onset of teenagehood (Thirteen). In most cases, there is a connection with their past where bullying abuse and teasing can be traced back. A child who is shy may end up becoming uneasy in their social life in their adult life which is also similar to children from parents who are domineering. There are also conditions which may happen in regard to our health. They may make our voices and appearances to be noted. This can also be a trigger for someone with an anger problem.

Lots of people with anger also exhibit a number of issues concerning their health. This may include depression, generalized panic attacks, or disorders of the dimorphic in the body.

When to get help for anger

Taking a step to go to your specialist when you feel your anger is getting the better part of you is a wise decision. Being overwhelmed by anger is not an out-of-place problem but has beneficial therapies that work. Though you may find it difficult to reach out and seek help, you will be surprised that it's a challenge that more than the average number of people have. Your therapist, if experienced, knows many people have an anger problem and thus will attempt to ease down your anxiety. He or she will ask several questions such as, how you feel when angry, what makes you angry, is there a place you go and do you begin to feel angry? All these questions are geared towards determining the magnitude of your anger. If they think you could have anger issues, you'll be referred to a mental health specialist to have a full assessment and weigh the treatment options. Moreover, you can also recommend yourself directly for mental therapies without seeing your doctor.

How you can overcome social stress

Anger is very tasking to handle even though some steps and actions that you take can lead you to the initiative to try. Furthermore, there is also a wide variety of medical options and treatments as well as support groups that are quite beneficial.

Things you can try

Individually helping yourself may not, in most cases, remedy anger. The anger may subside and it is equally a major step towards finding more helpful ways. Let us see what other steps we can undertake:

- By first analyzing what you think about before you get angry and the action you take after gives you a clear view of what challenges you are facing.
- At the time, you may feel a certain situation did not happen as planned. Be reasonable about it and you may conclude what you had planned was impractical.

- Get the attention away from your mind and yourself. Focus it on other people. You will realize the social challenges you are having are not apparent.

- Start involving yourself in what you would naturally keep off. You can do it in small doses, then progress as you feel comfortable about it.

Remedies to cure panic socially

Some primary examples include:

1. Through a professional therapist who uses a remedy that is both behavioral and cognitive. This remedy is helpful in enabling you to recognize behaviors and patterns that have a negative impact on your behavior.

2. Using individual help. By using a course downloaded from the internet or through a workbook and sufficient one-on-one help from a professional therapist.

3. Anti-depressant medicine. This is a type of medicine called a picky serotonin reuptake inhibitor or SSRI. The commonly known options are escitalopram or sertraline.

CBT is thought to be the best option for treatment, even though other modes of treatment are effective in case it does not give the desired results or you are not keen to undergo the therapy. Other individuals, however, respond well when several treatments are combined.

How is anger treated?

First of all, visit your general physician or healthcare specialist about how you feel. Your practitioner will carry out a test and ask questions regarding your health over the past period. This is done to rule out any other problem that may not be responsible for your current mental health status. Then they will refer you to either a doctor who specializes in mental health or a counselor. They will get to understand the underlying factors that lead to your current mental issues.

Anger is usually treated with psychotherapy, which is at times referred to as "talk" or face-to-face therapy, whereby medicine can be added or not. It's important to openly discuss with your doctor what treatment is fit for you and any adverse reactions you should expect.

Support Groups

A number of individuals prefer being with like-minded or with people facing similar challenges as what they are facing. In these groups, they find support and are given feedback to any questions that have without being judged wrongly. In these groups, they also get to hear how other people handle their anxieties in a social setting and may be inclined to try out. In doing so, they feel they are not the only ones going through that challenge, and hence, motivated to keep on achieving good and better results through their effort.

Psychotherapy

There is a category of psychiatric therapy that is both behavioral and cognitive and is very helpful in the treatment of anger. It has a variety of ways that one can think, act, and react to circumstances that make you end up feeling less worried and at ease. It also enables you to enhance your skills in your social life. When this therapy is done in a group setting, the results are remarkable.

Medicine Used

The medicines used to treat disorders that are as a result of stress socially are only three, namely:

- Anti-anger medications

- Antidepressants

- Beta-blockers

Anti-anger medications work in a powerful way and have an immediate effect on reducing feelings of uneasiness. Nonetheless, such medicine is not recommended for use for long periods. This is because as patients get used to them, they may require excessive dosages so as to get the preferred effect. In order to keep away from such problems, doctors prefer giving it for a short length and older patients are mostly preferred for these dosages.

Anti-depressants. Though they mainly work for individuals who are depressed, they also do well in tackling anger symptoms. Unlike anti-anger medicines, depressants take a number of weeks before they work. They also have various side effects such as sleeping difficulty, headache, and nausea. Although these effects are not severe for individuals whose dosage is gradually increased, it is always important to contact your health provider in case of any undesirable drug outcome.

Beta-blockers medications enable the prevention of a number of signs that occur physically. These include body tremors, an increase in heart rate, and perspiration. Beta-blockers are mostly used for the "performance anger" which is also a category of anger.

By working closely with your medical caregiver, you will find the most suitable medicine for you. A larger part of the population finds out that they get better results when different medications and other psychotherapies are used. As you discuss the dosage and length of treatment, bear in mind it might take a bit longer, so be prepared psychologically for the long haul. This helps in not giving up on treatment.

Remember to not only rely on the medications but check how healthy your lifestyle is and make any positive changes that need to be made. For example, if you do not exercise, get some time and start and let it be regular. Getting adequate sleep and reaching out to your family and friends when you need someone to talk or support you will give you positive results in the long run.

Treatment Options

There are various treatments for anger difficulties though they may affect each individual differently. While a few may require a single option, others do well when various options are combined. Your general healthcare physician will refer you to a mental care provider if they deem so and in regard to your symptoms and treatment needed. The various treatment alternatives include:

Cognitive Behavioral Therapy

This therapy is useful as it enables one to have control over their thoughts when angry via taking in short breaths and generally relaxing. The thoughts are geared towards being positive hence the anger is controlled.

Exposure therapy

When using this therapy, you gradually gain the courage to face situations in your social life that you avoided or felt coerced to be involved..

Group therapy

This therapy is for people who need to feel at ease in social gatherings, as they acquire the skills and techniques needed to be able to socialize and interact with others. Being a participant in a group opens you to the reality of not being alone in tackling anger issues. You also get a chance to showcase what you have learned before going out and meeting different people in different settings.

Treatments that one can do at home include:

1. Staying away from coffee

Caffeine drinks, as well as chocolate, are body stimulants and they may trigger anger. Soft drinks are also not recommended.

2. Having a lot of sleep

When individuals do not get enough sleep, their irritation levels heighten and they might not be very pleasant to be around. Getting enough sleep preferably for eight hours is highly commendable.

Just like many other mental health conditions, anger condition is also likely to arise from the interaction of various factors which include both environmental and natural.

These causes are:

> Qualities may be inherited down generations and in some cases, anger issues stand out. Although this observation is not fully clear as to what degree people inherit anger genes or is the anger they portray learned from childhood.

> A feature in the brain. Amygdala is a part of the brain that is responsible for how we respond to various circumstances. Individuals whose amygdala is highly active may be easily triggered into anger.

> Anger learned from our surroundings. Some individuals grow up in homes where there are heightened anger levels, so they learn what it is to be angry and how to react. There may be a connection between domineering parents and anger issues in children.

The Dangers

Anger can be encouraged through the following factors:

- ***Background.*** You have higher chances of developing anger in case your birth parents and siblings had the same issues.

- ***Unfavorable encounter.*** Individuals who are teased, bullied, rejected, ridiculed, or humiliated may be more vulnerable to anger. Additionally, other undesired occasions such as conflicts between family members, abuse, or trauma are anger linked.

- ***Temperament.*** Kids who are withdrawn in different and unfamiliar circumstances are highly vulnerable.

- ***Demands made by changing social life and work.*** Signs of anger basically kick in during teenagehood, although being in unfamiliar territory like reading a speech for the first time in public may provoke anger signs.

Complications

If left untreated, anger can ruin your life. Anger disorders can interrupt one's personal relationships, work, and school or other joys of anger. Anger is also responsible for:

> Shallow self-assurance

> Problem with being confident and firm.

> Talk about oneself negatively

> Very sensitive to any kind of criticism

> Inadequate competence socially

> Solitude including lack of skills to engage with peers

> Below average in work and academic achievements.

> Abusing of alcohol and alcohol-related products.

> Have a tendency of trying to commit suicide.

How to avoid the above complications:

There are various ways to help us cope, and hopefully, avoid the above complications. In doing the following, we will also be keeping away from having anger-related problems.

- Getting help earlier. Procrastination is one of the greatest enemies of dealing with anger issues. This is because as anger continues to affect your mental health, other areas of your life also suffer certain effects.

- Keeping record. Tracking your daily reactions in different circumstances and places will help you have a clear record as to how you can handle anger issues in your life.

- Get your priorities organized and be mentally prepared to follow through. This will enable you to feel in control and you are also able to engage and use your energy in what you enjoy. Thus anger issues will stay at bay.

Avoid anything that is addictive and harmful to your health. These include alcoholic drinks, drugs, nicotine, and caffeine. Though quitting may not be easy, you can consult with your health provider or even join a similar support group that will help you.

Chapter 6: Anger Management and Emotional Intelligence

What is Nonviolent Communication?

Human beings cannot live in isolation. We are a social species, and we need interaction and communication with other human beings for our sustenance. For us, connections with other human beings are not just a convenience but essentiality for survival. Communication is the most basic need of any social group including animals. Every animal species has its way of communicating and talking with each other.

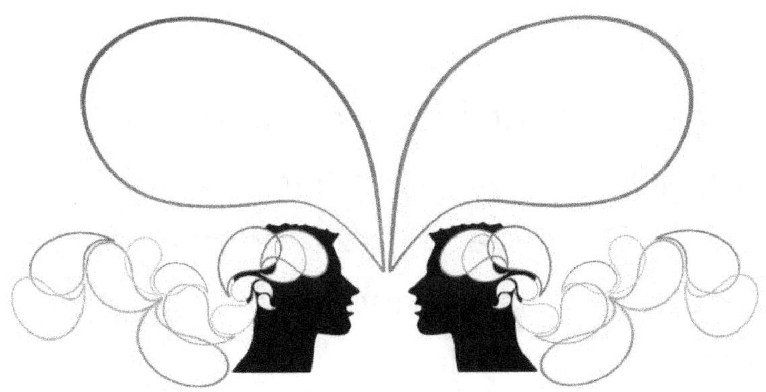

Therefore, communication is a two-way process by which thoughts, ideas, and emotions are exchanged meaningfully. Talking to people gives us happiness and joy. Talking to people also makes us feel sad, angry, and resentful. What is the difference between the two types of talking? What is it in the process of communication that affects how we feel?

Violent Vs. Nonviolent Communication

What kinds of communication make us happy and joyful and what kinds make us sad, angry, and hurt? Violent communication creates sadness and hurtful feelings whereas nonviolent communication creates joy and happiness for everyone involved in the discussion. Violent communication can include a range of elements including:

> ➢ Judging and criticizing people, deciding good/bad behavior, right/wrong people and situations
> ➢ Having prejudicial views based on race, gender, caste, creed, nationality, or anything else
> ➢ Discriminatory behavior
> ➢ Finger-pointing and blaming
> ➢ Talking without listening

- ➢ Reacting negatively when angry
- ➢ Name-calling
- ➢ Using rhetoric
- ➢ Being defensive

Any conversation or interaction with one or more of the elements mentioned in the above list is bound to result in violent communication.

So, what is nonviolent communication (NVC)? It is a form of empathetic communication that is based on the belief that every human being is capable of compassion. Nonviolent communication is deeply rooted in compassion. Marshall B. Rosenberg, the founder of the Center of Nonviolent Communication (CNVC), believed that being compassionate is the natural state of being for all humans. It is natural to find joy and happiness in giving and receiving from the heart.

If this is true, what is it that disconnects us from our natural state of compassion and makes us behave exploitatively and violently? Also, what is it that helps us remain in this natural state of compassion even in worst-case scenarios? One of the biggest factors that affect our compassionate nature is language and communication. Many times, even if we don't appear to talk violently in the physical sense, our choice of words can make an interaction violent inasmuch it causes pain and hurt to others, and that is referred to as violent communication, too.

Why do we indulge in this kind of communication style? Dr. Marshall Rosenberg said that this is because we are trained to perceive and speak judgmentally, labeling elements as right or wrong, and evaluating things in ways that disconnect us from our natural compassionate nature. Nonviolent communication is an approach that teaches us to give and receive from our hearts so that we are reconnected to our natural state of compassion.

NVC helps us to overcome automatic, habitual reactions, and responses and choose to express ourselves objectively and non-judgmentally by being conscious of our behaviors, feelings, and choice of words. NVC helps us to express ourselves honestly and clearly even, as we listen and pay attention to others' emotions and opinions empathetically and respectfully.

In any interaction based on nonviolent communication, not only are we aware of our deep needs and desires but also conscious of other people's needs and desires. By careful observations, we are able to specify external conditions and internal thoughts and emotions that are affecting our behaviors, and then make appropriate changes to our communication style that facilitates compassion and understanding for ourselves and fellow human beings.

Nonviolent communication is a combination of four elements or components including consciousness, language, communication skills, and means of influence. Let us look at each of these four elements of nonviolent communication in detail.

Consciousness – An individual who displays consciousness in his or her communication holds four human values high in their life; collaboration, compassion, authenticity, and courage.

Language – A nonviolent communicator is one who understands the importance and value of words and how they can increase or decrease distances and connections between people.

Communication skills – Nonviolent communicators have excellent communication skills. Such people:

> ➢ Know how to ask for what they want
>
> ➢ Know how to listen to others even in disagreements
>
> ➢ Know who to collaborate with and find solutions that work well for all stakeholders

Means of influence – Nonviolent communicators accept and acknowledge the importance of 'sharing power' instead of 'using power over others.'

Nonviolent communication helps us to live with deep connections with people and sensible choices based on facts enabling you to live a meaningful and happy life.

Marshall B. Rosenberg said, *"Human beings are powerhouses of joy and happiness, and each one of us is capable of enriching lives through our words and interactions with other people. We can have great support. We can nurture. We can contribute and participate in other people's enjoyment. On the other hand, we also have the power to make people miserable through our words and actions. It is up to us to make the right choice of learning the various aspects of nonviolent communication to enrich our lives and those of others."*

How is NVC different from other self-help, communication, and conflict management tools? - The uniqueness of nonviolent communication can be found in the following elements:

Assumptions of NVC are unique – The start of NVC itself is beautiful and unique. This communication self-help tool assumes that every human being is capable of compassion and love. We are all nonviolent by nature, and violence is a learned behavior supported by or taught by external circumstances, including but not limited to the prevailing culture and norm. Another important assumption of NVC is that all human beings have the same primary needs, and all our actions, reactions, and responses are used to meet these basic human needs.

The NVC tool is simple to learn and use – The process involved in using the NVC tool is simple to learn and master and equally simple to implement in our daily lives. The crucial thing about NVC is that it is not merely a communication tool. NVC techniques teach us how to stay connected with our life energy. It improves our consciousness by making us focus on how our thinking and communication impacts our daily conversations.

NVC can be applied effectively for a wide variety of purposes and needs – The use of NVC techniques is not restricted to any one or two communication needs. You can effectively use NVC techniques on a wide range of needs ranging from personal, professional, business, interpersonal, family, parenting, sibling, and more. It also helps to overcome social issues such as alcoholism, substance abuse, recovery from trauma, and prisoner rehabilitation.

NVC promises amazing results – NVC techniques can transform destructive attitudes such as anger, resentment, and more. It helps you break destructive habits and convert them into life-serving and peaceful behaviors. NVC has been used all over the world to reduce conflicts in families and business organizations, increase trust, and foster deep emotional connections to benefit all stakeholders.

Benefits of Learning Non-violent Communication

Learning the skills of nonviolent communication helps you with the following:

Conflict resolution

Nonviolent communication methods teach you to resolve all kinds of conflicts amicably. You will be able to get to the root of the dispute quickly, and effectively help you find solutions. With nonviolent communication, you will learn to improve your listening skills significantly which allows you to get enhanced levels of cooperation from the different people you deal with.

Nonviolent communication skills help you convert criticism and blame into a compassionate understanding of the other person's point of view. With the help of all these conflict resolution skills, your ability to reduce misunderstandings and prevent pain from similar mistakes both for yourself and the people around will improve considerably.

Improved personal relationships

NVC is great for personal relationships. Being skilled in nonviolent communication helps you deepen your emotional connections with other people. Your improved listening skills will increase cooperative interactions with your family and friends. You will find ways to get what you want without the use of guilt or shame.

Improved family relationship

With NVC, you will reduce sibling rivalry and family conflicts and you will be able to help people in your family to go beyond power struggles towards an attitude of cooperation and trust. NVC teaches you the power of using unconditional love to bring a family together. As a parent, you will be able to nurture your children without stepping on their sense of autonomy and freedom. NVC skills teach you to motivate by sharing power with loved ones rather than using power over them.

The improved education system and better students

NVC helps us to optimize the potential of each student and strengthen their passion, interest, dedication, and connection to learning and development. NVC skills help to improve connection and trust in the classroom and empower them to feel safe and secure. NVC helps to improve efficiency and cooperation among students and enhance teamwork in the classroom while strengthening the power of parent-teacher relationships; a key ingredient in the overall development of a student.

Self-healing and personal growth

NVC empowers you to change guilt and shame into learning elements. It helps you heal old, festering pains and also facilitates the elimination of old, limiting habits and thoughts. NVC helps you to remain connected with your desires, preferences, and needs. It teaches you how to cultivate the habit of eating by choice and not by habit; a crucial item for physical health.

Organizational effectiveness

NVC improves the productivity and effectiveness of meetings. Also, employees will feel an increased sense of morale, confidence, and team spirit, helping them improve their productivity for organizational effectiveness and development. NVC helps you optimize the quality of work and also the social benefits of your company to the community and society.

Anger management

NVC helps you redirect your anger productively before it can drive damaging behavior. NVC enables you to identify and understand the needs of your anger, the triggers that drive angry behavior both for yourself and others. NVC helps you overcome the challenges of anger and facilitates solution-driven proactive behavior instead of regretful reactions. With nonviolent communication, you will find ways to express your anger without harming anyone.

Business relationships

NVC helps in building employee loyalty and morale by helping them achieve their optimum potential. With NVC, you will find ways to resolve workplace conflicts effectively and with little or no residual damage. It reduces absenteeism and stress in the workplace. It helps in improved customer relationships by understanding and preempting their needs and requirements.

Spirituality

NVC helps you connect to your inner being. You will find that with NVC you are able to align your actions with your spiritual values and moral principles helping you lead a wholesome and meaningful life. NVC helps you overcome conditioned harmful behavior developed from your cultural background and connect with the whole of humanity. NVC helps you understand that identifying and satisfying your own needs is the first step to building compassion for others. You can also reap all these benefits and more by learning and implementing NVC techniques in your life.

The Four-Step Nonviolent Communication Process

To reiterate one part of what was already said in the introduction chapter, the primary premise on which Nonviolent communication (NVC) works is that all human beings have the same basic needs. One of the most important human need is the sense that they are being listened to, understood, respected, and valued.

NVC techniques are all designed to have meaningful conversations that connect to everyone's needs, and not to 'win' or 'lose'. The four-step communication process of NVC includes:

Observations

A neutral way of observing what is happening inside and outside of you is the first and foremost step in the NVC four-step process. In a conversation, this is best done by recapping what has been said by others without attaching any emotion to it. When you recap or summarize a person's conversation, it is imperative not to be judgmental about the 'story'. Recapping what the other person is saying helps in the following ways:

- It slows down the conversation giving everyone time to rethink and reconsider their understanding and interpretations. The person whose idea you are recapping feels that he or she is being listened to and understood; one of the most important human needs.

- Recapping helps people to enhance their memory about the conversation helping them recall it better in the future.

- It helps to catch and correct errors. When we are talking fast and without a stop, it is natural for all of us to make mistakes in the form of misplaced words or phrases that mean something quite different from what we actually wanted to say. Recapping helps in catching and correcting these mistakes. Recapping acts like an editing process of what was spoken earlier.

Recapping works extremely well when you use the first person. Instead of starting with 'You said that,' it would be better starting with, 'I hear what you are saying....' Here are some examples of recapping:

Suppose your husband walks in and says, "Oh God! These immigrants have come into our country and are taking our jobs away." Your response would be, "Did something happen in the office today that is making you feel insecure about your job? Would you want to talk about that incidence?"

Notice, by recapping what your husband said, not only did you let him know that you were listening to what he was saying but also catch the underlying fears about something that happened in the office that day. Your recapping of his statements has made him think about what he said which, in turn, will slow down his speed of thoughts giving him the necessary time to really comprehend his emotions and feelings. He is forced to reflect on what he said, and clarify his stance. Moreover, he feels a sense of connection with you, and he is ready to discuss the issue without letting the fears affect his judgment.

Feelings

The next step in the NVC four-step process is to describe and focus on the emotions and feelings, and not the situation. If you want to be heard, then you must describe your feelings and emotions, and not just what is happening because everyone can easily see what it is. What they cannot see are your feelings and emotions which makes it important that you reveal them through words.

The crucial aspect of expressing your emotions is to ensure not to make it feel like you are blaming someone or something. For example, if you say, "I feel misunderstood...' it could translate to someone not making an effort to understand you resulting in transferring or laying blame on others.

"I feel good about what happened," or "I feel bad about what happened," is talking about your feelings. Similarly, asking someone, 'How do you feel about what happened?' instead of simply asking, 'What happened?' will shift the focus from the situation to the person's feelings and interpretation. This makes people feel like they are being heard, and their concerns are being addressed.

Needs and Requests

The third step in the NVC four-step process is to identify the need behind the feelings or emotions. This approach is based on one of the assumptions of NVC which is that we all experience emotions because of an underlying need. So, the next step after identifying the feeling is to discern and identify it.

Human beings feel a sense of dissatisfaction leading to anger and resentment when we have unmet needs. Interestingly, the founder of NVC, Marshall B. Rosenberg noticed that nearly all human needs could fit into a small list of categories including honesty, connection, and peace, a sense of purpose, physical well-being, and autonomy.

Identifying needs is the turning point in conflict resolution. You can ask questions that will bring the underlying need of the other person's emotions to the surface. For example, you can say, 'Can you tell me exactly what your concerns are and from where do these concerns arise?'

Similarly, when you are talking about your unmet need, you must explicitly express the problem. For example, in that husband-wife conversation, if the husband had said something like this, 'I am worried about job security if people are allowed to migrate without restriction,' would have immediately reflected the unmet human need of peace and well-being.

In any conversation, if two people are talking without understanding the drive and motivation of the other person, then the resultant conversation will look like two overflowing glasses of water with no space to hold anything more. In order to understand any person's perspective, you must first empty your mind so that there is space for what the other individual is trying to put in.

The Importance of Unlearning Old Lessons

Here is a beautiful Zen Buddhist story that illustrates the need to empty our biases to understand and appreciate someone else's point of view. A highly learned professor went to a master to learn Zen. As the master was filling the professor's teacup, the professor was continuously talking about what he knew and had heard about the subject.

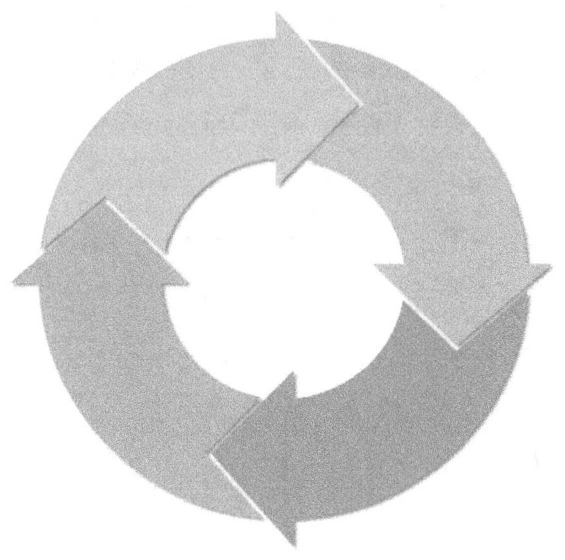

The master listened without saying a word and poured tea into the professor's cup until it reaches the brim. However, the master did not stop here. He continued to pour the liquid resulting in the cup overflowing. The professor watched this strange action for some time, and then abruptly stopped talking about Zen, and told the master, 'Stop pouring. The cup cannot hold anything more.'

The Zen master replied, 'You are like the teacup. Unless you empty your cup, how will I fill it with what I know of Zen?' So, first, empty your mind, and only then are you ready to receive more.

Every situation can be seen through this four-step process which can then be used to improve your communication style effectively. Here is an example that explains the use of the 4-step nonviolent communication.

Sharon's mother, Denise, is feeling quite frustrated with her daughter's annoying habit of bundling her socks into balls and throwing them all over the house instead of putting them either in the washing machine or the laundry basket. She has tried all the traditional methods of communicating her anger and annoyance; by screaming, cajoling, bribing, etc. Nothing has worked. So, Denise now decided to use the 4-step process of nonviolent communication.

Observations – First, she observes everything around her and the external conditions. Denise keeps out words like 'annoying,' 'frustrated,' etc. Instead, she observes everything in a non-judgmental manner. She notices the mess that the balled-up socks create in the living room, kitchen, etc. and these are common areas in the home used by other members of the family too.

Feelings – Next, she looks at how she is feeling and recognizes and identifies some of the top emotions she is experiencing. Denise is frustrated, angry, and feels helpless.

Needs – Denise then looks at her underlying need in this entire situation. She needs the common spaces to look clean at all times so that everyone in the house can get together without any feeling of discomfort brought about by the odor of smelly socks.

Requests – After following the three steps, she words her communication like this: Sharon, I can see three balls of socks under the dining table, and two balls of rolled-up socks under the settee in the living room. It angers me to see these lying around in the common area of the home because this space needs more order than your bedroom as everyone in the family accesses and uses it. Can I request you to put your used socks either in the laundry basket or the washing machine from now onwards?

The last sentence is the request part of the NVC process that has to be delivered so that others can clearly and unequivocally understand our needs. These needs are the ones that enrich our lives, and nonviolent communication is the way that helps each of us achieve our needs using our natural feeling of compassion to give and receive from the depths of our hearts.

Chapter 7: Mental Disorder, the Origin of Problems

What is mental health?

According to WHO (World Health Organization), health, which includes mental health, involves a state of entire mental, physical, and social well-being, which means it's not just about the absence of a disease or condition.

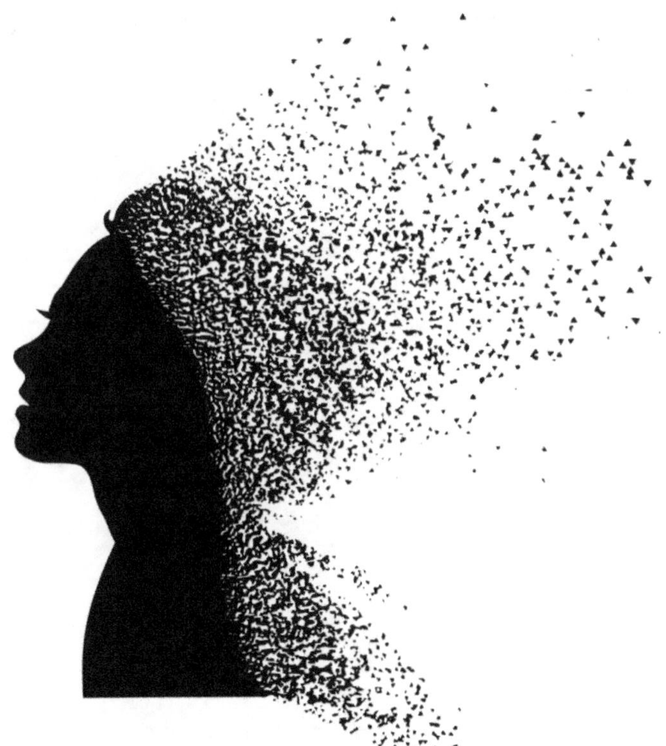

The same definition applies to proper mental health, which implies it's not just about the presence or absence of mental disorders such as anxiety and depression, or bipolar disorders, amongst others. If one is mentally healthy, then it means they are aware of their own capabilities, can cope with life's normal dramas, and will work effectively in a bid to make a mark on his or her community.

We can, therefore, say that good mental health is the core of the effectiveness of an individual and the community around him or her.

In the name of good mental health

CBT has done a great job of making people realize themselves and be able to get back on track. It has been used to treat several conditions (you can refer to the Introduction to see what CBT can be used to address).

On the other hand, mental health involves more than one strategy if we need to make sure that positivity stays in us on a long-term basis. Promoting good mental health involves utilizing strategies and prepared programs that generate an enabling environment that has the right living conditions for people to abide by and be able to maintain healthy conditions.

There is no particular program aimed at mental health, and that is why it will involve more than CBT. The range of programs available should be thanked by those who have benefited, since one specific measure may not suit your troubled neighbor. They all give us a chance to enjoy the fruits of staying positive by allowing the mind to adjust the way it thinks.

What determines your state of mental health?

Mental health has a range of factors that influence it, which is the same as physical health. The factors are also interactive, and they include psychological, biological, and social aspects. Research has shown that the evidence is well portrayed in poverty, low or improper education, low income earning, or poor housing and sanitation.

The declining socioeconomic status that has more disadvantages will force individuals to succumb to mental disorders. Those who are more vulnerable involve the less fortunate or disadvantaged and within a community prone to mental disorders. If other additional factors such as insecurity, hopelessness, poor body health, increased risks of violence, and rapid social change are also around, that also partially explains why we may be having improper mental health.

Ways that you can use to promote overall psychological wellbeing

Here are some things to consider as you look forward to reinstating good mental health.

Look for what is affecting you

Since we aren't the same, it is crucial that you investigate your individual causes of ill mental health. On the other hand, some shared causes may be becoming stressed, or depressed, finding difficulty in coping or quit something, or generally upset. There are life events that may affect our mental health. They include:

- ➢ Being lonely
- ➢ Loss of someone close to you
- ➢ Illicit relationships
- ➢ Financial issues
- ➢ Work-related problems

NB: loneliness, insomnia, stress, and inactivity are all forms of negativity when it comes to mental wellbeing. At times, it is almost impossible to determine why we experience mental disorders. While it is a cause to worry, there are other factors that will lead to such feelings. They maybe happened or occurred in the past.

They may involve the following:

- ➤ Neglect, child abuse, or violence
- ➤ Homelessness, especially for those who have experienced foster care
- ➤ Social discrimination
- ➤ Terminal illness in us or in the family
- ➤ Loss of a job or unemployment
- ➤ Poverty and debt
- ➤ Trauma associated with life experiences such as high-level crime, military issues, or being involved in major tragedies such as bomb attacks

Regardless of the cause, what you need to remember is that you have a right to feel great and there is a protocol for you to achieve that.

Building relationships that can help you

Getting involved in social groups or having a friend will give you a sense of belonging if it's not yet there. It will help you cope with difficulty if you manage to do the following:

Connect with loved ones: Always keep in touch with your friends and relatives with the convenient method available. You can plan to visit, call them, or leave them messages.

Joining social groups: What do you like to do? Some of us like playing instruments, others drawing, swimming, and the list is endless.

Talk about your feelings: If you have someone that you can trust with your personal issues, it's a good idea to open up to them. It also shows that you are aware of what is happening to you, so explaining it to someone actually helps. At times, it is hard to explain it to our friends, but you can do that to a person who has a similar experience. If you have a chance, please utilize it. There are online groups that one can join in expressing and try to solve mental matters.

Make time for yourself

It can appear selfish to set time for yourself, but it is vital to your overall wellbeing and can help you spring out from mental difficulty.

Mindfulness: Having your presence helps you to realize oneself and be able to manage what we feel. The goal here is to enjoy life again and accept what is around you. We will cover this in detail in the next chapter.

Acquire a new skill: If you learn something that you have been longing for, or will help you later, it gives you the confidence and the joy of achievement. You could sign up for a class or try a new language. Whatever it is, it doesn't have to be big.

Relaxing techniques: Do something that soothes your mind such as having a bath, listening to music, or going for a jog. All these and more will help you cope with stress and mental disorders.

Examine your mental health status

If you are already aware of your mental condition or difficulty, take the appropriate steps to make sure that you are improving.

Talk about what will help you: If there is a strategy that worked on you before, tell the one helping you out. Let those close to you know what can support you better such as listening to your troubles or making you aware of your issues.

Stay alert for warning signs: If you can be aware of how you feel and are able to spot signs that depict you are unwell, that is much better. Being aware of such signs will help you when it becomes hectic, and it will also form the base guidance to those who are directing and supporting you.

Use a mood diary: Just like we track our daily activities, we can also record our moods, and we have seen that is possible in the previous chapters. Have a way to record your moods, the negative issues that you think of, and ways to help you stay positive. If you have no idea how to write one, there are online sources to help you with that such as <u>moodscope.com</u>

Upgrade your self-esteem: It is one of the major steps in making yourself ready to challenge your mental issues.

Physical health is vital to mental wellbeing

Look after your body and what you are subjecting it to. Here are a few recommended things:

Eating healthy

> - Invest in a well-balanced diet
> - Eat regularly so that your energy levels are constant, and the body can regulate sugar levels
> - Have fruits and vegetables aplenty
> - Avoid alcohol and other drugs that ruin the mental ability

Moving it

Engage in exercise to keep the juices flowing, which will also help you get rid of negativity. Some activities include:

> - A walk
> - Bike riding
> - Swimming
> - Yoga
> - Football
> - Martial arts

Have enough sleep

Tiredness brings in more worry and stress. Doctors' orders direct you to sleep 8 hours per day.

> ➢ Have a bedtime routine, such as drinking milk or hot water before sleeping. Later, you can read a book or listen to music that helps you sleep.
> ➢ Sleep and wake up at the same time every day.
> ➢ Do not drink anything caffeinated after lunch.

As we wrap up this chapter, it is important to consider other methods that will help you gain better mental health as you continue with CBT. That way, you will have more tools to conquer what you need to get rid of.

Chapter 8: How to Increase your Self-Awareness

Self-Awareness and Emotional Intelligence

Let us assume a situation that is happening in your professional life. You own a small website-building firm that is doing reasonably good business. You have five employees working for you, and your professional life is well on its path to becoming a big success.

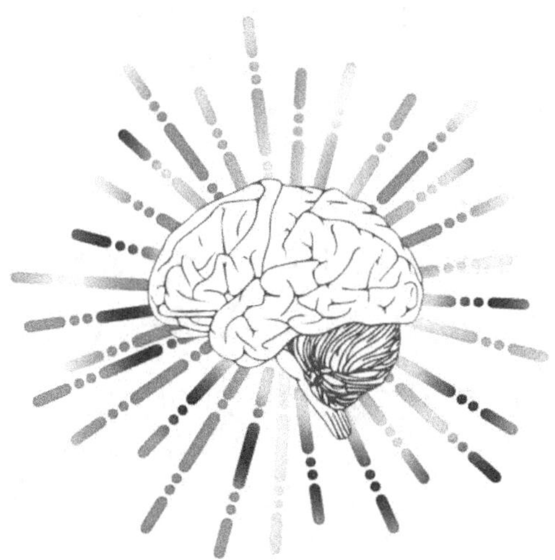

It is a clear Monday morning; sunny skies and all your employees have turned out. Your accountant prints out last week's sales figures and you are happy with the numbers. The present week also promises to bring in some good business. Everything seems hunky-dory, and you are feeling happy and good. There are no major strong emotions in your system currently.

Suddenly, your phone rings and one of your topmost clients; one who contributes to nearly 20% of your business is on the line. He is furious because his website has stopped working, and he has lost a lot of business because of this, and he blames you for it and threatens to take away his business unless you find a way to correct the mistakes right away. In that spur of a moment, you become acutely aware of the following:

- Your heart is beating fast.
- Your hands are all clammy with sweat.
- You are unable even to form words of apology.
- You almost drop your phone.

You become aware that you are now anxious and the calm feeling you had a couple of minutes ago has gone! This is the most basic form of self-awareness which is a simple phrase to explain a complex network of information and data about your feelings, your thoughts, and all the things happening to you.

Self-awareness is a measure of how well you know yourself at different levels including the senses of your physical body, emotions, intentions, preferences, goals and desires, how you are perceived by other people, and more. The higher your level of self-awareness, the easier it is to find ways to adapt yourself to different situations and requirements. And the better we can adapt our responses and reactions to the people in our lives, the more satisfying our relationships will be.

We are constantly bombarded by messages from all over the globe, and yet we know so little about our own selves. We don't know how to set up a conversation with ourselves and build our self-awareness. And when we don't know ourselves well, we fall short of understanding other people too. Our inability to recognize and identify our emotions reduces our ability to respond appropriately and in ways that meet everyone's needs.

Therefore, increasing your self-awareness is a crucial element to improving emotional intelligence. All emotions and feelings are nothing but bytes of data made up of energy. All types of emotions are giving us information of some sort. Even unpleasant emotions give us valuable information. Therefore, emotions are always positive when it comes to how much we can learn from them. The more we tune in to our emotions, the healthier we become by leveraging the power of the data provided by the feelings.

Being Aware Of Your Emotions AND Expressing Them

Yes, expressing your emotions is quite a different matter from being aware of them. How we express our emotions, or even whether we express them at all, is our deliberate choice. However, making the right choice regarding emotional expressions first requires you to be aware of them, to know they exist, and the physical and mental feelings they bring with them. Once we become aware of our emotions, then an entire gamut of how we can express them opens up, and you can choose what suits you the best at that particular point in time.

Reacting to emotions without being aware of them are automatic, and are neither guided by intuition nor by reason. Suppose you start your day with some negative experience. The unpleasantness of that bitter experience will invariably spill on to the day, and you will show your unhappiness and negative behavior right through the day without even knowing that these negativities are the residual effects of the morning unpleasantness.

Then, someone who cares for you and knows you well walk into your cabin and reminds you of your irritable state of mind right from the morning. That is the first time you are made aware of your feelings and emotions and their root cause. We are, in effect, startled into a state of awareness. Once we 'experience' our emotions, then our brains are wired into this experience, and it uses this new data to find ways to overcome your negativity. This new information gained by our brain through our awareness of the feelings is used to look at things from a positive perspective which was not visible before we became 'aware' of that nasty emotion.

The lack of self-awareness also can be damaging because you could have reached the brink, and if you still are not aware, then wittingly or not someone is going to push you over the brink. This situation happens because a limbic memory (something beyond our control) has been triggered, and we end up using responses learned earlier during our childhood days such as shrinking from our boss when he or she shouts at us just like how we behaved during our childhood days when some strict elder in the house or teacher in school screamed at us for some wrongdoing.

The lack of self-awareness results in the loss of self-control. Therefore, self-awareness is the first step to get back control of your life and empower yourself to react and respond appropriately. This self-control and the freedom to behave as you wish are the pillars that hold up the power of empathy and genuine concern for fellow-beings.

Most of the time, we are unaware of our emotions until such time they become very strong. It is important to know that just like how we are always thinking something (our thoughts never stop), we are always feeling something. Just like how we have to become acutely aware of our thoughts to be more intelligent, we have to become acutely aware of our emotions to become emotionally intelligent. We should learn to feel and experience our emotions.

Self-Awareness and Nonviolent Communication

Let us look at the four components of nonviolent communication through the lens of self-awareness and understand the connection between the two. The four pillars of nonviolent communication include observation, feelings, needs, and requests.

Observations and Self-Awareness

What is observation? It is our ability to discern the various stimuli that are driving our reactions and responses. The sight of a cute baby gurgling with laughter brings a smile to our faces. The sight of an image depicting a starving child in a remote famine-ridden place fills our heart with sadness, and many times, such powerful images can involuntarily bring tears in our eyes.

Observation is what we see, hear, feel, and sense the different stimuli within us and in our surroundings. The purpose of self-awareness is to be accurately aware and describe what we are reacting to or responding to. The trick in self-awareness is to be aware of everything that is taking place at any point in time neutrally and objectively. You must be like a video camera that is merely capturing everything that is happening at the point in time without judging.

What we observe neutrally and specifically gives us the context for our reactions, responses, and the expressions of emotions and needs. The key element in building good observational skills is to be able to separate your own opinions and judgments from the description of the stimuli, and this attitude and approach are what will help in creating and maintaining nonviolent communication with everyone around us.

For instance, if we said, 'You were rude to me,' to someone, that person is quite likely to disagree with us. However, if we said, 'When you walked into the room, I noticed that you did not greet me,' they are more likely to agree with you because your description of the observation was accurate, objective, and did not include your own interpretation.

When we describe our observation in this way without mixing up our feelings in the description, the person you are speaking to is quite likely to involve himself or herself in this first stage of the conversation without reacting negatively, and more willing to move towards the feelings and needs aspect of the communication process.

Therefore, by becoming more self-aware, you learn to translate your own opinions, interpretations, and judgments into an objective observational language. This approach helps to move away from our feelings of right/wrong. Consequently, we will find it easy to take responsibility for our actions because this objective outlook will direct our attention to the fact that our feelings are a result of our needs, and does not have anything to do with the other person(s).

Therefore, building observation skills helps us develop increased self-awareness, helping us get closer to our true selves. Increased self-awareness builds our relationships and connections with other people as well, and our overall consciousness will shift towards becoming more authentic than before.

Feelings and Self-Awareness

What are the feelings? They represent our collective physical sensations and emotional experiences connected to our met and/or unmet needs. Self-awareness is our ability to identify and label these feelings, again without judgment. It is important to focus on words that express the feeling and emotion instead of focusing on words that express our interpretations and opinions on the actions of other people.

Here is an example to illustrate the above point; telling your partner 'I feel lonely,' describes your feeling. However, if you said, 'I feel that you don't like me anymore,' is a description of your interpretation of your partner's behavior. Expressing your feelings is continuing to take responsibility for your actions and your experiences.

Here is another example to illustrate how increased self-awareness about your feelings and emotions can help you manage difficult situations. Suppose your new team member goofed up big time on a very important project that is due in a week.

It is true that you are angry with him or she for the mistake committed. However, if you include your own feeling of anxiety about completing the project well and on time, then your reaction to the person's faults will be more wholesome, and you will be in a better frame of mind to help the new person to correct the errors and still meet the deadline.

Consequently, the listener gets to hear about your feelings without the burden of having to take blame, criticism, or responsibility for your experiences. This kind of situation enhances the chances of the outcome of the communication process to meet the needs of everyone concerned.

Identifying and labeling emotions is a critical step to building self-awareness, improving your nonviolent communication capabilities, and increasing your emotional intelligence. Remember, there are no good or bad emotions; there are only emotions. Yes, some of the feelings may appear to be more pleasant to experience than others. However, every emotion is giving you valuable information, and self-awareness helps you discern this valuable information.

Also, feelings need not always accurately reflect the situation. It is possible for you to feel guilty even when you know you have done no wrong or feel a sense of panic when there is really nothing to fear or a sense of joy even in a toxic relationship. Even misplaced emotions are communicating something important to you.

For example, if you are feeling unduly guilty, then maybe it is time for you to start creating boundaries for yourself and reducing other people's expectations from you. Feelings of misplaced fear could be an indication that this is new territory for you, and you will benefit from the learning.

All this can happen only when you become increasingly aware of your feelings, and delve deep into your psyche to try and analyze them, and see whether or not they fit into the situation that created them in the first place. Here are some feelings and what they might convey to you. Remember, this list is only a guideline to get you started on increasing your self-awareness about your feelings. You could build your own set of guidelines as you become increasingly aware of how your emotions play out. Also, remember the intensity of the emotions is telling you something.

Love – Love could be telling you that something (or everything) about a particular relationship or situation is going well.

Grief – Sadness or grief is an indication that you need love and succor from others. It is important to listen to this emotion and reach out for help because unresolved grief can lead to disastrous outcomes.

Guilt – Guilt is typically an indicator of some mistake we have done. You can use guilt to correct mistakes. Undue guilt could be an indication that you have let others raise their expectations from you excessively.

Shame – Perhaps, one of the most unpleasant emotions to go through, shame also has a purpose. The biggest disadvantage of feeling shame is that it makes us feel inadequate and flawed, and these negative feelings could drive us to go into hiding which is counterproductive to solving problems.

For example, if you are ashamed of being overweight, then not being socially active could be a way of hiding this feeling. Identifying and labeling this emotion is the first step to correcting such faulty beliefs, and finding ways to overcome challenges that are creating the feeling of shame in you.

Anger – This is a powerful emotion that tells us that we have been wronged. The most basic reaction would be to either confront the person who is the cause of your anger or simply speak to someone you trust and express your anger openly. Accumulating anger is one of the most debilitating ways of handling this potent feeling. You can channelize anger into productive work.

Anxiety – There are two types of anxiety namely productive and non-productive. The productive anxiety is giving you mature advice to remain on your guard and alert to get the best outcome for yourself to achieve all your dreams and desires. Non-productive anxiety, on the other hand, is debilitating to the point of not allowing you to do your regular daily tasks. It increases stress and reduces your ability to get things done effectively and efficiently.

Happiness – Like love, the feeling of true happiness is an indication that something is going right. Happiness can be felt even during difficult phases of your life. For example, if you have not had enough money to take your children out for a fancy Christmas dinner but have managed to cook up some amazing food for them at home, and they have that grateful smile on their faces despite their disappointment, you will feel happiness.

Needs and Self-Awareness

All human beings share critical survival needs including food, sleep, shelter, rest, and a desire to connect with other human beings. Other than these basic needs, we have other needs that we share. These needs are experienced by different people at varying degrees of intensity. Some of us need the feeling of connection more than others while some might have an increased need for self-esteem.

Moreover, in different situations, our needs could be different. For example, when at home, one individual might need the attention of his or her spouse more than anything else while at the workplace, the same person might not need the attention of other people.

Self-awareness is to be totally aware of these deep longings that form the foundation of our life purposes. When we are deeply aware of these longings, then we are able to connect to ourselves in a much better way than before which in turn helps us build better relationships with other people. Being aware of our needs helps us behave and act in ways that meet everyone's needs.

Most often, we express our wants and needs through a strategy of asking for something from someone. For example, 'Please come to my birthday party,' is a specific strategy that reflects your need for love and companionship on that special day. Once you shift your focus from the strategy to the underlying need, then you liberate yourself from finding having to limit the ways of meeting that need. You are ready to explore other alternatives. Moreover, when you become aware of the fact that everything you do or say reflects an underlying need, then you will also learn to understand that the same holds good for others as well.

When needs are met or unmet, feelings arise. Feelings are triggered by our experience associated with the unmet or met needs; positive if met and negative if unmet. When we connect our feelings to our needs, we take responsibility for our emotions resulting in blame-free and criticism-free relationships with others.

Requests and Self-Awareness

Requests represent strategies that help us meet our needs. Identifying and accepting this deep connection between requests and needs will enhance our self-awareness. Quite often, in any given moment in time, the responses of other people to our requests are based on our connection with them. For example, if you ask someone, 'What do you think of this?" their response to your question is dependent on your connection with them then.

The most important element of creating strategies through requests is to be ready to take 'no' for an answer and continue to seek out alternative solutions either on your own or with the help of others. A critical difference between a demand and a request lies in our response to a situation when the other person denies our request/demand. In the case of demand, a denial typically leads to conflict or some other sort of punitive consequence whereas a denied request usually leads to further dialogue.

In a requested scenario, a 'no' is nothing but an expression of some unmet need for the other person which is preventing him or her from saying 'yes'.

Increased self-awareness will alert you to the fact that saying 'yes' to your request is proving very costly for the other person, and a bit of negotiation is in order to make sure that both your needs are met.

Here is a classic example of how to discern between an undoable demand and a doable request that meets the needs of everyone concerned. Suppose you have an employee who has a problem with coming late. One way of ensuring discipline is by saying, 'I want you to be on time to the office consistently.'

However, this is undoable because obviously, there is some his of need that is being unmet which is why he is not able to come on time. Moreover, he is bound to come up with some excuse each day even after promising to be on time due to other unmet needs that were not resolved with your undoable demand.

Instead, if you told him, 'Can you spare me 15 minutes so that we can discuss how we can help each other to make sure you don't come late to the office every day?' Now, this request is doable because not only is your need for time discipline met but also the employee's needs of confidence, connection, trust, respect, responsibility, etc. This willingness to work together to meet everyone's needs is a sign of high emotional intelligence and a key differentiator of a highly self-aware individual.

Tips to Build Self-Awareness

So, how can you build your level of self-awareness to develop your emotional intelligence and nonviolent communication skills? Here are some tips for that:

See yourself objectively – When you see yourself objectively, it is easier to come to terms with your weaknesses and feel proud of your strengths without bordering on arrogance. For example, think of your current situation, and write down your thoughts. Here are some prompts:

- What are you good at?
- What do you need to improve on?
- What are the accomplishments are you proud of?
- What are the things that could you have done better?
- What are the happy memories of your childhood? What has changed since then, and why?

Seek out people whom you trust and ask for honest feedback – Knowing yourself also means knowing how other people perceive you. This can be quite a challenge because most people find it difficult to give honest feedback. The ones who dislike you will be critical of your every effort, and those who like you might not want to hurt you by giving criticisms.

It is only those who truly love and care for you will give you honest, upfront feedback; using which you can progress in your self-awareness journey. Keep track of such people, and always keep them in your life.

Maintain a journal – Write down your thoughts in a journal as often as you can. Doing it every day before you go to bed is the most effective way of looking back on your day objectively, as you note down the events and your accompanying thoughts and feelings.

However, sometimes, during highly emotional periods, you might want to write down your intense emotions immediately. Don't hesitate to make a note in little chits of paper. This action of transferring your thoughts into a written form is a great way to release the emotion-driven stress from your system. Make sure you write down both the good and bad things that took place during the day.

Also, write down your needs, plans, goals, and priorities. Thoughts are nebulous and putting them down into words and saving them on paper is the best way to read and learn from your experiences later on.

Allocate some time for self-reflection – Increasing self-awareness means you have to be with yourself for some time. Use this alone time for self-reflection. Don't skim the surfaces of your emotions. Dig deep and ask yourself why you are so happy. Don't feel ashamed to face your jealousy and other weaknesses. There is nothing wrong with having flaws. What is wrong is not finding the courage to fight them and overcome them.

Focus on your breath – Get away from the hustle and bustle of your daily life for at least 15 minutes each day. Choose any convenient time. Find a quiet, undisturbed, and comfortable spot. Sit down, and close your eyes. Now, observe how you breathe.

Don't try and control it. Simply observe the inhalation and exhalation process. Your thoughts are bound to wander away. Bring your mind gently to focus on your breath. Initially, 15 minutes will seem like a long time. However, soon you will find that you feel more connected to yourself than before. You are comfortable being alone with your thoughts. You like solitude.

Practice mindfulness – Mindfulness is the science of 'living in the moment' so that you experience and engage with life fully. Immerse yourself in every action you are performing. Focusing on your breath is a deliberate mindfulness exercise. Here are some more.

For example, when you eat your meals, the current trend is to watch TV or carry on a conversation with other people. For your next meal, focus only on eating your meal. Take small bites. Chew at least 20 times before swallowing. Focus and feel the flavor, texture, and taste of the food. Don't focus on whether you like it or not. Simply focus on the sensations in your mouth and tongue.

When you are walking, focus on the sensations on your legs, how the calf muscles, ankles, and other parts of your legs are moving. Focus on your breathing. Is it very fast or is it slow? Don't try to control it. Simply observe all your feelings and sensations.

Slowly, with practice, you will find yourself becoming increasingly productive and efficient because your entire being is focused on this one act. You will find yourself being able to recognize every feeling your body senses as you eat, sleep, walk, wash dishes, breathe, etc.

These are some of the most basic methods of developing self-awareness. The more self-aware you are, the better control you have over how you choose to react and respond to your emotions.

Chapter 9: Mindfulness, Use Mindfulness Techniques when you are Angry

Alertness is to purposefully mind about an occurrence as it unfolds. These happen as we watch but without us imposing any of our comments and not having a vague idea of how it should turn out. It is a healthy way which enables us to respond to what we are experiencing. In addition, we able to conquer the tendencies of our mind that are not intended and hence protects us from feeling we did not get what we wanted.

The practice of meditation is a fundamental technique for the development of mindfulness. Meditating has its own mental and physical effects which enable our ability to naturally become aware of the eternity in us. It is also a transparency of our persona to face what is real without being biased. When alertness and meditating are faced through this vain, then letting go of former expectations, ideas, and opinions we may have formed about this subject. These happen in both the physical and metaphysical areas.

Over time, two moral standards of discipline that is empathy and wisdom are built up. When we able to see clearly the fundamental reality of nature then that is wisdom.

We can practice being alert. Any individual can use these techniques to perform the simple areas of life such as talking sensing, feeling, breathing, and even driving.

Mindfulness in Practice

If like most people, you get upset and annoyed with yourself for feeling disturbed, edgy, or panicky and in response to your frustrations, you try to resist these feelings, you'll soon realize that you are only strengthening these negative emotions and making them worse than they already are. What you should do instead of resisting your feelings is just to allow yourself to feel the way you are feeling. Learning to accept this will help a great deal and it will eventually settle down and pass.

Here are three fundamental and brief mindfulness techniques that you can apply to help you find a release from worry, anxiety, and a panic attack before it escalates.

Anchoring

One of the best ways to quiet yourself down is to ground yourself. Yes, ground yourself. In other words "anchor yourself." You can achieve this by channeling the totality of your thoughts and attention into the lower half of your body.

> To begin, focus your attention on your feet. Concentrate on how they feel inside your socks or shoes. Pay attention to the hardness of the ground against them.

> Now that you have a complete focus on your feet, allow that focus to move from your lower legs and gradually through your upper legs. Savor the sensation. How does it feel? Dense or feathery? Toasty or chilly? Exited or paralyzed?

> To conclude the process, feel yourself inhale, exhale, and relax as you continue the breathing process.

This is an extraordinary method of anchoring yourself. It is something you can practice at any time, having your eyes open or closed, in a seated position or even while moving around. It is easy: anchor yourself and then breathes.

Breathe Counting

The mind is always busy, recounting stories, translating our experience by filling in missing snippets of information, and afterward, ruminating over the stories it has created, whether they are actually true or false.

This method can either be utilized in conjunction with anchoring or utilized alone.

> ➢ The first step is anchoring. Count up to "6", as you inhale deeply the next time you breathe in.
> ➢ Then count up to "10" as you exhale.

This strategy has the impact of protracting both the in-breath and the out-breath, thereby slowing down your breathing. It additionally lengthens the out-breath more than the in-breath, driving you to discharge more carbon dioxide, slowing your pulse, calming you down, and re-establishing emotional equilibrium.

Ensure you fit the numbers to your breath and not the other way around. On the off chance that 6 and 10 don't work for you, discover another proportion that works, provided that the out-breath is longer than the in-breath with a minimum of two counts. You can count for one full breath, then take one normal breath and count the next one if it becomes too difficult to continue breathing at the same time as counting.

In the event that you can't manage counting because you feel panicked, then as you breathe in, say to yourself, "in" and as you breathe out, say, "out" completely, endeavoring to extend the out-breath. Repeat the process for at least one minute, or you can go for whatever length of time that you require. This method can be cast-off very effectively to charge off approaching panic outbreaks at night.

'Finger Breathing'

This is another version of 'breathe counting.' The following are the procedures of the above subject:

- ➢ Bring one of your hands in front of you with the palm facing towards you.
- ➢ Trail up the outer length of your thumb by the index finger of your extra hand whereas you breathe in. Break at the peak point of your thumb and now dash it quickly on the other on the side while you breathe out. That's a single breath.
- ➢ Keep an eye on up the side of the ensuing finger while you draw in. Recess at the top and, later, trace down the extra side of that finger as you respire. Those are now two breaths.
- ➢ Continue outlining along every finger as you tally every breath. Move back up the preceding finger after the accomplishment of the end of the finger and reprise the practice in reverse.

This exercise is extremely valuable when there is a lot going on around you, and you find it difficult to close your eyes and focus inwards. It gives you something visual to focus on, something kinesthetic to do with your hands, and it also helps you focus on counting and your breathing. This is a very simple procedure to teach young people and children.

Doodling

Doodling is an incredible tool to activate your celestial creative self. When combined with the power of Mandala, it can help you access profound parts of your brain through these steps.

> Draw a dot at the center of your canvas /paper. This dot represents the seed of an idea you want to expand on and get innovative with. Everything creative started with a basic seed. It's like the Big Bang.

> Next, you develop your idea and your creativity by drawing 4 lines out from the dot, each line pointing toward north, south, east, and west, respectively.

> Continue expanding your idea by drawing the next 4 lines out from the dot, which will look like lines extending NE, SE, SW, and NW.

> Draw a petal on each line. The petals represent your personal, creative development.

> Draw a heart in the middle of each petal and a circle around the lines.

> Then, again, draw a heart in between every two petals

- ➤ Now draw a circle around the entire center. This speaks to advance creativity and growth within the circles you have made with the networks and connections you have framed.
- ➤ Draw a dot that connects each line with the circle, then, on the circle, draw 8 dots. This depicts co-creation within your connections and networks and planting seeds of growth along the way.
- ➤ Draw the image for the lotus petal, joining each dot.
- ➤ Inside each lotus petal, make a sketch of any preferred symbol (the symbol must be similar). Make a sketch of a symbol that represents something significant to you, such as a flower, a musical note, or maybe a football, inside the lotus flower. What you doodle doesn't matter. Make a doodle of anything that comes to your mind. That's your mandala!

There is no restriction on how big or how much you draw so you can keep expanding out and including details Bear in mind, however, that it won't be perfect, but it will be lovely!

Coloring

This is similar to doodling

> ➤ Keep it artless. Start with a blank page and a color.

> ➤ Start with a figure that you find stress-free to draw. For instance, a loop. Remember to retain it simple.

> ➤ Draw form after form, and believe your instinct. Perhaps make a bunch of rounds together.

> ➤ If you think there should be limited lines, go forward and do it. Make those outlines. Get silly.

> ➤ Give yourself the approval to put whatever you want on the page. You can fill the sheet as far as conceivable, or halt when you have a longing for faltering. Simply keep up with it till you feel done.

> ➤ Get your day feeling revitalized. The simple turn of sketching on a page can do miracles.

The most vibrant thing is to quiet your thoughts. On the occasion that you discover yourself being tense and distressing that you are not doing it correctly, simply grasp a deep gasp and let that self-deprecation go. The goal is to attain a nice of Zen state, where you're only giving your hand an opportunity to make scripts, and your brain to have contemplation without verdict while you're not really thinking about no matter what in precise.

These mindfulness techniques are not new. They have been utilized by many psychologists and counselors for years. The fact that we can all benefit from these techniques and the fact that they are effective for everyday experiences is a relatively new discovery. Try them and notice what happens.

Chapter 10: Cognitive Behavioral Therapy

What is Cognitive Behavioral Therapy (CBT)?

Mental health is paramount in the way we conduct ourselves. That is why CBT (Cognitive Behavioral Therapy) takes a step to change how we think, the beliefs that hold us back knowingly or unknowingly, our attitude towards various issues affecting our lives, and how we behave when facing challenging situations, not forgetting to strive to achieve our set objectives.

Adjusting your negative thoughts using this form of therapy does not need to take your whole lifetime. Those who receive it from their therapists know that it takes utmost, ten months with 50-60 minutes per session once a week. While we can view it as a hands-on approach that requires you and the professional to be available, sometimes it's overwhelming to see you juggle your mind in front of someone who is continuously looking at their watch.

That is why we give you a solution that you can use while at home.

This does not mean that you should ignore professional help when presented. If you can read and are able to identify what is troubling your mind, therapists may not be necessary after going to that quiet spot a few times a week just like in therapy.

A Little History about Cognitive Behavioral Therapy

Aaron Beck is the name behind this form of therapy. In the '60s, this man was busy working on psychoanalysis on his patients. During the analysis, he noted something strange and unusual. They seemed to have an *inner dialogue* going on in their minds as if they had someone else talking to them in there or were merely talking to themselves internally. When Beck enquired about their thinking status, the patients only produced a portion of the total information.

To give an example, the patient in his office was probably thinking, "The therapist is super quiet today. Am I boring him or does he have a lot on his mind to ponder?" The first sentence of thought triggered the second one, and this is how such an internal dialogue starts. After some time, the client would think, "Maybe my issues are not that important to this high-end figure." At this point, he or she will not adequately communicate their real feelings.

That is when Beck came to know that something connected one's feelings and thoughts. He went ahead to come up with the phrase *automatic thoughts* to signify the ideas overwhelmed by emotions that come abruptly to mind without the knowledge of the victim. While it may not be possible for the client to know what is happening in their brain, there is a way to identify them and report when they occur.

By identifying such thinking modes, the client would then be able to understand what is happening to them and eventually overcome the hurdles in life.

That is when Cognitive Behavioral Therapy was born. The primary purpose was to place the importance of thinking about the forefront of solving our problems. The terms cognitive and behavior are joined together since apart from the mind, behavioral techniques also need to be addressed. A balance between the two varies depending on other forms of therapy using CBT as the main basis, but they are all defined under this form of treatment. Today, it has undergone various professional trials all over the world in a bid to solve mind and behavior-related problems.

Cognitive Behavioral Therapy in Depth

Cognitive Behavioral Therapy represents a goal-oriented psychological therapy treatment whose hands-on approach drives towards problem-solving. The objective here is to change our thinking patterns or the behavioral aspects that bring about the difficulties which will eventually replace the focus of our feelings. If you looked at the introduction, there are many problems that this form of therapy can address, from sleeping troubles to anxiety, depression, and drug abuse.

Using CBT means finding a way to change the patient's attitude and how they respond to situations by shedding light on the beliefs, images, and thoughts held in the cognitive process. In that way, the victim can focus and be able to deal with emotional situations.

Think of it as a combination of behavioral therapy and psychotherapy. The latter focuses on the meaning we use on what we come across in our lives and how the thinking pattern started when we were little. Behavioral therapy, on the other hand, digs into the relationship available between our thoughts and problems and how we behave.

The following diagram will show you how the things mentioned above are interconnected. We will then focus on it by applying various life situations that will pick the same pattern as depicted below.

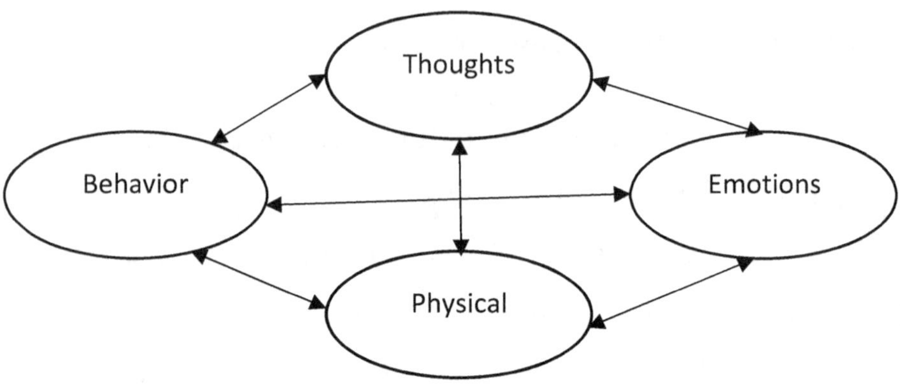

CBT Principles

Since it includes learning essential skills that will help us manage what makes us feel down, you will possess new methods of behaving and thinking as you look forward to controlling your situation in the future. Here are a few things you need to understand when using CBT.

This form of therapy focuses on the present

We must dig into the past to get the cause of what is happening to us. On the other hand, CBT treatment will focus on the symptoms that are currently driving you in the wrong direction and not where it all began. So, for example, if you are dealing with anxiety, knowing where it all started is not enough to help you cope.

Homework is essential

Whether it comes from a therapist or this self-help book, homework is vital. Doing the assignments given means that you will have something to do every week and you need to practice what you learn by applying the skills daily? Since it is homework, you need to keep using what you have gained until it sticks in your mind.

Necessitating the need for practice is not enough, so you need something more than motivation. Unless you learn to practice the things you have learned, what is most likely to happen is that you'll forget after some time. When you are later facing your problem, it will be hard to remember how to utilize the skills.

Learning the new methods can be compared to gaining a new habit, healthy to be precise. If you need to start jogging in the morning, it might appear hard in the first few days, but after a few trials, it will become part of your routine. CBT applies the same notion. If you make it a habit to practice what will make you change the way you think and act, you'll soon get used to it. So, the more you are into it, the easier it gets.

Are There Pros And Cons In CBT?

While it is as effective as the medication used when treating valid mental disorders, one man's meat is another man's poison, so it may not suit every psychologically-driven behavior. The advantages include:

> Time taken can be relatively shorter than other forms of therapy consume.

> It can be the only solution where medication is not working.

> There are many ways of presenting it, which include using a therapist, getting self-help books, or using apps.

> The skills taught are practical when applied in everyday life even after therapy.

The disadvantages include:

> - There is a need for more cooperation and commitment since it is a long process.
> - Much time consumption especially if it involves a therapist and extra work to be done.
> - There is a confrontation of emotions and thoughts here so, during the beginning, one is bound to experience some uncomfortable form of anxiety.
> - Complex mental issues may need further assistance and treatment. At such a point, CBT may not be of good use.

This Is What You Need To Remember

> - CBT is research-based, so there is proof that it works.
> - CBT teaches us new thinking and behaving ways. This is a self-help book that can help you with that.
> - What we think, feel, and behave are all in a cycle, so they are interconnected. Changing one means affecting the rest.

Chapter 11: Meditation Techniques

The Power of Meditation and Relaxation to Ease Anger

The word meditation originates from the Latin word 'meditatio' and means to think, ponder or contemplate. Meditation is a way of transforming the mind and body through techniques that enhance and develop concentration and positivity. It is a method of deep relaxation that rests the mind and in turn the body.

Simply put, meditation is the peace of mind!

The aim of meditation is to achieve self-regulation of the mind by using the various meditation techniques for relaxation, mental clarity and building positive internal energy. It is this end that helps to manage health problems like anger, depression and high blood pressure.

The body is nourished and healed through rest. Deep rest and relaxation achieved through meditation are, therefore, great for rejuvenating the body to leave you well and mentally serene. Research has shown that the degree of rest achieved when one is meditating is greater than that harnessed from sleep. The findings are incredible. 20 minutes of deep meditation has been equated to 7 hours of sleep!

The desired goal of mental clarity, positivity, and peace are reached through a regular practice of meditative techniques. For maximum harvest of the benefits, be committed to this art. In the course of time, your body will get into a rhythm and in tune for inner peace.

Types or Techniques of Meditation

There are many different types and techniques of meditation that we shall not be able to cover everything. Meditative techniques are in the hundreds but are all linked by the common thread of aiming at achieving inner peace for the practitioner.

First and foremost, all meditative practices engage in mind control techniques as a way to achieve relaxation and peace. Secondly, there are postures and body movements that are found in all forms of meditation. These two traits are evident in all meditative practices pointing to a common goal for all of them.

Meditation helps to relieve our bodies and minds of the toxic effects of stress, relaxes us and brings the peace of mind that we all yearn for. Before you pick up one form of meditation or another, it is important to do your research and learn as much as you can about them. Interrogate yourself, find out and decide what your meditative goals are or would be to help you pick up the right technique for you.

In some cases, you will need to get a teacher or join a meditation school for the right advice, coaching, and mentorship in taking up meditation. There are types of meditative practices that cannot be performed by beginners, people with certain conditions or illnesses or older people for example. Seeking the right information will guide you to the right technique. It is also important to remember to take on a meditative practice that will fit your lifestyle. Meditation requires consistency, regularity, discipline, and high commitment for one to realize the desired fruits. With the many types of meditation in existence, we can generally categorize meditation as follows:

1. Concentrative Meditation

In concentrative meditation, the mind is directed to a particular object, chant/mantra, sound, or sensation. The practitioner will focus their mind and energy on a focal point of their choosing that best works for them in an effort to clear and calm their minds and bodies. These types of meditations are good for beginners.

2. Mindfulness Meditation

This type of meditation does not rely on focusing the mind on an object but relies on feelings, sensations, emotions and thought patterns to achieve a meditative state. These are more advanced types of meditation that are not for everyone especially beginners.

3. Effortless Transcending

This is another form of reflection that is referred to as "effortless". This is because no effort is needed to perform it mentally. It is also called "pure being", "transcendental". This form seeks to calm you as you meditate inwards and empty yourself of any hindrance. This enables the practitioner to recognize their true essence by emptying or eliminating all their thoughts.

With consistent practice, our souls are an open space that allows for relaxation. It has been compared to massaging the brain. The transcendental process will help the practitioner be in a silent zone where they are aware of their deepest state of being conscious. Individuals who practice this type of alertness testify of finding the great feelings in the experience.

Below are various reflections

4. Buddhist meditation

a) Zen Meditation (Zazen)

Zazen is Japanese meaning "seated Zen" or "seated meditation"- referring to the form of Zen meditation practiced while sitting. Zazen originates from Chinese Zen Buddhism. It is done while seated on the floor usually on a mat with crossed legs and was traditionally done in the lotus or half-lotus position.

For the mind, Zazen employs two techniques:

- Focus on breathing. The practitioner will pay attention to inhalation and exhalation will silently counting down with every breath and back.

- Shikantanza. Here, there is no specific object of meditation. One remains in the moment being aware of what goes through their mind and what passes around.

b) *Vipassana Meditation*

Vipassana means clear seeing or insight and is a Buddhist type of meditation. It is ideal for mental discovery and awareness. It starts with mindfulness of breath to stabilize and focus the mind –focused mind meditation. Then it moves to develop clarity of awareness of bodily sensations and mental phenomena. Sit on the floor legs crossed with a straight back.

5. Mindfulness Meditation

Mindfulness meditation combines practices from various Buddhist meditation practices. It is widely employed in hospitals and other health benefits as a form of treatment. Here, the practitioner will focus on the moment while not losing awareness of thoughts and emotions experienced.

6. Religious/Spiritual Meditation

These are meditative practices that are practiced among different religions. Remember that spirituality is one avenue for achieving peace of mind and relaxation. Here, meditation and prayer are combined to achieve spiritual development by the reflection of God's word. Meditation is a communion with the self with the aim of spiritual development or divinity.

Meditation in religion is practiced for peace of mind by steadying and focusing it on giving the practitioner the ability for divine insight. A practitioner of Christian meditation said that God is sought through the study of scripture but through meditation, he is found. There are forms of meditative practices in almost all religions which prove the close link between spirituality and meditation.

Sufism meditative practices are some of the most elaborate of religious meditation. Practitioners get into a rhythm of chanting and movement that eventually transports participants into a spiritual realm. In Christianity, there are examples with the Catholics and Orthodox sects that have mantras or repetitive prayers.

7. Metta Meditation

It is also referred to as loving-kindness meditation and has its roots in Tibet. This meditative form enhances empathy and compassion to make one more loving to self and others. The practitioner will sit and close their eyes, then generate feelings of kindness and compassion in their mind towards themselves then progress to others. Just like the name suggests, this type of meditation aims at creating harmony with one's surroundings. Treat all things with kindness and the rewards are happiness and compassion for you. You emit happiness and the world bounces it back to you.

8. Hindu Meditations

Vedic and Yogic forms of meditation are Hindu forms and are classified as follows:

Mantra Meditation- Mantra involves the repetition of a word or phrase to focus on one's mind.

Transcendental Meditation- Transcendental techniques aim at opening the mind.

Yoga Meditation- Yoga means union and there are many types. Yoga combines mind relaxing and focusing on practices with stretching movements and postures. Of all the meditative practices, yoga is the most popular of the secular forms of meditation and has the most following for non-religious or spiritual meditation. You will find that most people who meditate are practicing one form of yoga or another.

How then do we use these techniques for self-improvement and relaxation? Let us first know the benefits of meditation.

Benefits of Meditation

There are several benefits apart from the ones we have discussed in the preceding sections. It is no wonder then that meditation is being promoted as an alternative to clinical treatment for cure and management of several health conditions and for general wellbeing. Meditation leads the body to undergo a change. Cells in the body are injected with more energy resulting in peace, happiness and motivation as the energy levels in the body are boosted

The benefits of meditative practices are:

- ➤ Meditation reverses or reduces the production of stress hormones (adrenaline) by creating calmness and eradicating anger to prevent chronic stress. With controlled or regulated stress hormones, the body is more relaxed.

- ➤ It is good for managing blood pressure and other heart diseases or conditions since the heart rate and breathing is slowed down. When we are not stressed, worried or anxious, the heart rate is slow therefore the blood pressure is also low. Meditation can help greatly with conditions like high blood pressure since it works to create calmness and relaxation.

> Boosts the immune system and slows aging as a result of less production of adrenaline by the body. The immune system is boosted since one ends up being healthier as a result of the suppression of destructive stress chemicals.

> Meditation brings clarity to the mind and creativity is enhanced. With a relaxed mind, one is sure to be more creative and productive.

> Meditative techniques advocate for a pure life and in fact, the aim of meditation is to attain purity akin to the higher being, so practitioners find themselves quitting poisonous habits like smoking, drug abuse, and alcohol consumption.

> Brain functioning is greatly improved through the boosting of psychological creativity, better memory, and a settled relaxed mind.

> Meditation makes you happier since your mind and body feel better. A relaxed person has no worries and will be a happier person.

➢ You will sleep better since you are relaxed, enabling you to have more rest and better rest to face the day and tasks that you are faced with.

➢ Reduces how fast we age through mental and physical exercise. People who meditate have a slower aging process. Stress hormones hasten aging while meditation is known to halt or significantly reduce their production.

➢ Meditation reduces or eliminates stress. A meditation practitioner is a calm and happy individual who is essentially immune to the effects of stress.

➢ A relaxed and happier person has the benefit of a better functioning body. Immunity is boosted and diseases are kept at bay.

➢ When one embraces meditation with all its tenets and understands it, they hold life to a greater value since they learn the true meaning and purpose of living.

➢ Meditative exercises improve metabolism and help regulate weight by fighting obesity.

- ➢ Meditation helps you feel more connected and in tune with yourself.

- ➢ Meditation brings emotional balance and harmony.

- ➢ Personal transformation is inevitable with meditation. You end up being a new person.

It is recommended that you meditate at least once in a day for optimal results –dawn meditation is highly recommended usually between 3 am to 6 am. Dawn meditation is considered more beneficial as you tend to be more alert and well-rested after your sleep. The environment is also quiet and ideal for meditation. In the next part, we shall learn how to use meditation to reduce stress in your life.

How to reduce Stress by Meditating

So, what is stress? Stress is basically the body's way of responding to pressure that may be exerted on it physically or psychologically. Stress is caused when the body releases stress chemicals usually adrenaline into the blood in an effort to combat whatever pressure it is confronted with. Stress can be classified as follows:

> Survival stress. This is stress that we face when we are confronted by dangerous situations where you feel that physical harm is imminent. It is here where we have a fight-and-flight response to fight stress.

> Internal stress. This is stress caused by worries over things that are out of your control. Simply put, internal stress is self-imposed stress that can be avoided by not giving yourself so much pressure over things that are beyond you.

> Environmental stress. This is stress caused by factors in your surroundings like noise etc. Stay away from environmental stress triggers and you have a happy life.

- Tiredness. This type of stress is caused by fatigue which usually accumulates over a long period of time due to such things as overworking.

Stress is an inescapable part of life and sooner or later we experience it. What we need to do is learn how to manage it so that it does not overwhelm us and take over our lives. Stress is not an entirely bad thing as it can enhance our alertness and concentration. However, in excess, it is very unhealthy.

Symptoms of stress

How do you know if you are stressed? The following are some signs that will let you know if you are stressed:

Cognitive symptoms

- Problems remembering things

- Low concentration

- High anger

- Constant worry

Emotional symptoms

- ➢ Being moody

- ➢ Highly irritable and angry

- ➢ Loneliness and reclusion

- ➢ Sadness

Physical symptoms

- ➢ Low libido

- ➢ Aches and pain

- ➢ High heart rate

- ➢ Dizziness

Behavioral symptoms

- ➢ Eating disorders. Bingeing or self-starving

- ➢ Lack of sleep

- ➢ Substance abuse

- ➢ Nervousness

Causes of stress

External causes

> Major life changes. Divorce, chronic illness, the death of a loved one

> Work burden

> Financial problems

> Trauma

Internal causes

> Constant worry

> Negativity and pessimism

> Fear and anger

> Unrealistic expectations

Stress can cause serious health and social problems if it is not dealt with immediately and well. Some of the side effects of stress are:

> Mental disorders like depression and anger

> Cardiovascular problems. High blood pressure, heart disease, stroke, etc.

> Weight problems such as obesity

> Problems with menstrual cycles

> Skin and hair problems such as acne, hair loss, etc.

> Sexual dysfunction

> Gastrointestinal problems like ulcers

Meditation and Stress Management

Meditation has been proven as a stress reliever and is being embraced by many for relaxation. Stress relief needs both mental and physical relaxation and meditation provides that. To understand why meditation is so helpful in reducing stress, we should know what it takes to relax:

Deep breathing

Deep breathing is a quick and sure way of deflating stress from your system; a simple technique with far-reaching positive consequences in keeping stress in check.

Balancing the nervous system

For the body to function optimally, the nervous system must be at equilibrium- you must be at peace mentally. Stress destabilizes this balance and the only way to stead your system is by relaxation. A state of profound serenity of the nervous system which is the counter to stress.

Using Meditation to achieve Relaxation

Relaxation is a state of mental and physical calmness and serenity where one is free from tension and anger. Meditation practices reduce muscle tension, lower blood pressure, calm the mind and eliminate stress in general. A response christened 'relaxation response' is elicited when the one is relaxed. It is the opposite of stress response experienced when one is under pressure. Meditation is one sure way of generating the relaxation response.

Regular meditation will regularly generate the relaxation response giving you more control of your body for a stress-free life. The following are the most used relaxation techniques:

- ***Progressive muscle relaxation***

This technique is used for relaxing deep muscle tension. Tension in the muscles increases anger and this technique will reduce muscle tension and lower the heart rate and blood pressure. It can be practiced while lying on your back or seated. You tense each muscle group for a few seconds and relaxed. This is repeated until the whole body relaxes.

- ***Deep breathing***

Deep breathing emphasizes breath control and focuses on your breathing to achieve a relaxed state. Take deep breathes from the stomach, breathing in enough air into your lungs. Deep breathes mean more oxygen into your system. More oxygen means less tension and anger. Deep breathing is simple but a powerful relaxation technique that is easily learned by all and can be done almost anywhere. It offers a quick fix for managing stress levels.

Remember that deep breathing is the basis of other relaxation techniques and can be applied together with other relaxation tools like aromatherapy and music. You can use the following routine for your deep breathing meditative technique:

- ➤ Sit with your back straight, a hand on your chest, and the other hand placed on your stomach. The hands should guide you through the breathing routine.
- ➤ Breathe in using your nose. The hand placed on your tummy will be pushed up while the other on your chest will move very little.

> Breathe out from your mouth, releasing the most air you can manage while constricting your stomach muscles. The hand placed on your stomach will move inwards as you breathe out while they will hardly move.

> Continue breathing in using your nose and exhaling through your mouth. Breathe in sufficient air so that your lower tummy rises and drops.

> Count down slowly as you breathe out.

> If breathing from your abdomen is a problem while you are seated, lie on a flat surface - the floor is ideal.

> Place a light visible object on your tummy to act as a guide and then breathe so that the object rises as you breathe in and falls as you breathe out.

Tense/Relax method - This technique is similar to progressive relaxation where you tense and relax muscles for relaxation.

***Autogenic method*-** The autogenic method is also about muscle control to make one calmer and relaxed.

Guided imagery or visualization method - This can be used in conjunction with progressive relaxation or by itself. After you have relaxed your muscles you can get into the visualization method and use mental imagery to relax your mind. Visualization method is a variation on traditional forms of meditation techniques that require that you use all senses; visual sense, of the palate, feel/touch, hearing, and smell. Visualization method entails the creation of an image in your mind which leaves you feeling at peace and free to release all tension and anger.

Self-hypnosis - Hypnotizing oneself is a form of meditation that is guided and participants listen to a recorded song or sound. By doing this, they are able to access and reach a state of deep relaxation as soon as possible. In this state, you are more open to suggestions giving the hypnotherapist the opportunity to target and improve a particular aspect of thought.

Standard meditation – Primarily, these are reflections that have particular guidance. They seek for particular aims and purposes. They are not similar to each other so you ought to know what you are using and where it is guiding you to.

Body scan - This is a reflection where the practitioner is guided on which part of their body to concentrate on. Then they are asked if they can identify anything. The practitioner has to be comfortable since it may take up to an hour even though shorter versions are available.

Brainwave meditation - This type of reflection targets brain waves for stress relief and relaxation. Brain wave meditations start out with a guiding voice, which is usually just relaxing sounds of music. Their aim is to keep the mind focused on the tunes.

Affirmation meditation - This meditative technique uses assurances to plant certain thoughts then generate particular feelings into a practitioner's mind. The practitioner's mind becomes at ease and they can be easily led to be more willing when in this state.

Every time you want to embark on a relaxation technique, do the following:

> ➤ Find a quiet spot where you will not be disturbed.

> ➤ Get into a comfortable position. Sitting or lying down.

> Loosen your clothes and free your arms and legs

> Dim your lights

Mastering these relaxation techniques will take time. Over time, your body will be in tune with the sequence of the relaxation techniques. With this mastery, you will be able to get deeper relaxation. Make these practices part of your lifestyle and do them daily. As much as it may be difficult to find exclusive time for meditation, these techniques can be put into practice as you engage in doing other things.

It is possible to meditate on a bus or while commuting for concentrative meditation. Mindfulness techniques can be put into play while walking or exercising your pet or while taking a lunch break at the park, etc. Nonetheless, if you can designate a daily time for relaxation, do so for predictability and ease. Do not try these relaxation techniques while sleepy, as you will fall asleep and miss out on your target for relaxation. Relaxation requires maximum concentration and alertness.

No one is perfect, especially at the beginning. Do not pinch yourself for missing some sessions. The main goal is to build momentum so that after a while, you can get into a rhythm and routine.

Peace of mind

Peace of mind is the key to true life. Happiness, good health, and success is something that should be accessed by every one of us. Meditation is one of the ways that you can attain the mental peace that will give you a wholesome life. When we look at the many benefits of meditative practices listed earlier, they refer to or are a testament to a state where one's body is in total control and fully functional.

Bad habits are jettisoned for a purer health-conscious one. Mental strength and brain functioning are greatly improved and nurtured. Immunity is boosted leading to fewer or no diseases affecting us. We are less stressed and a lot happier when we meditate regularly. This happiness and well-being are what spawns peace of mind. One becomes aware and in tune with themselves. Full self-awareness is achieved and with that comes the peace. When your mind is peaceful, you will be more productive and you will relate better with people around you. Your family, friends, colleagues at work and strangers that you bump into will notice the difference in how you relate. You become more likable, as the happiness and peace you exude rubs off onto others.

Meditation indeed leads to peace of mind. Take up meditation, won't you?

Quick and Simple Techniques for a Beginner's Practice

Now that you have all the basic knowledge you need, it is time to delve into the practice itself. There are many kinds of meditation techniques that you can get acquainted with, and this chapter will aim to give you as many options as possible to help you start strong.

Fast and Simple: Techniques on the Go

There are just too many people out there who don't have enough time in their hands but still want to practice meditation. Although meditation can be done anywhere and in almost any circumstance, it is important that you start with some beginner-friendly practices that won't take up too much time. All the exercises in this section can be done within 10 minutes, but you can make it last longer if you want.

When you are using certain techniques to fit a certain time frame, you have to put all thought of time constraints out of your head. It would be best if you chose a short time after you wake up or just before you go to bed. Keep in mind that making your mind be still is not easily accomplished, especially for a beginner. But also know that this can become simpler and easier as you go along, so don't let yourself be discouraged by any short-term setbacks.

Basic Meditation with Affirmation

This basic meditation technique is a great way to start your practice. This starts off with the basics and you can add visualizations or added stillness later on.

> ➤ Sit on the floor or on a chair and keep your back as straight as possible without straining yourself. Make sure that you are comfortable and can hold the position for at least five minutes. Choose a place where you won't be disturbed.

> ➤ Breathe deeply and relax your body as you breathe. As this is probably your first time, it might be wise to keep your eyes closed throughout the process.

> ➤ Choose a phrase that you would like to affirm in your life. Try and use the first person and make sure it's something meaningful to you. Examples can include "There is peace inside

me," "I am worthy of love," or "God watches over me."

➢ Take slow measured breaths. Make your breathing as easy and relaxed as possible and empty your mind of other thoughts.

➢ Now repeat the affirmation to yourself quietly. Try and focus only on the affirmation. If you do get distracted by random thoughts, allow the thought to pass rather than suppress it. Simply return your attention to the affirmation gently.

➢ If you find it difficult to focus on a purely mental effort, you can try and whisper the words to yourself, moving your tongue without really speaking a word. Join your breathing with your affirmation and repeat the phrase as you breathe out.

Continue this exercise for at least five minutes. Remember not to get frustrated, as your body will end up tensing rather than relaxing. Notice how you felt during the exercise. Was focusing your attention on affirmations and breathing difficult for you? What kinds of thoughts did you find popping into your head?

Focused Breathing

When you can manage to stay focused on affirmations, it is time you focus solely on the breath. This is a great way to develop focused awareness, concentration, and stillness of the mind. Don't expect to have a quiet mind right away. This is all normal and will improve as you continue your practice.

> Sit comfortably with your back straight in a place where you won't be disturbed.

> Breathe deeply and relax your body. You can choose to close your eyes or keep them open. However, if you find that your thoughts still have a tendency to race around you, keeping your eyes closed will help keep distractions at the minimal.

> Turn your attention towards the sensation of your breath. This is a good time to practice the beginner's mind. Experience your breathing as if for the first time. Feel your chest rise and fall as you breathe. Listen intently to the sound of each breath and feel the air enter and leave your body.

> Continue this meditation for at least five minutes. Since you are focusing solely on your breathing,

you might find yourself easily distracted by random thoughts and emotions. Don't be alarmed or critical of yourself when this happens. Simply acknowledge the thought or emotion without judgment, then let it go. Gently direct your focus back to your breathing.

It would be beneficial for you to continue practicing these techniques before you move on to more complex practices. As the basic core of almost all of the meditation practices involves awareness of the breath and concentration, these techniques are great if you simply want to stay with the basics or if you want to move on and deepen your practice.

Conclusion

Thank you for coming this far. If there is anything in life that everyone yearns for, it is great. The good thing is usually not just enough. You will always want to be great in everything you do. Be it coding, playing football, playing the violin, or even in writing. The key to being great at something is usually very simple—practicing. The practice is the habitual art of repeatedly exercising an activity so as to acquire perfection in it. Practicing the right way can really mean the difference between good and great.

Let's look first at the quantity of practice time. You might ask yourself, for how long should you practice something for you to perfect it? You might know some top athletes, footballers, or even musicians. They always have one thing in common. They usually put in lots of hours per day in perfecting their skills. The measure of perfection, therefore, is usually measured by how much time you put into the practice.

However, as much as practicing is all about repeatedly exercising an activity, taking too much time on an activity can lead to boredom. So, what is the upper limit to how much quantity of practice time is good? Many are the times when more is not better if it becomes too much. You should, therefore, be aware of the number of hours you need to practice activity so that you can acquire its perfection.

The upper limits, therefore, for the hours that you should practice in a day as an adult professional are four to five hours a day. These hours should be divided into sessions lasting not more than sixty to ninety minutes. Taking more time than this can lead to boredom, burn-out, and even lack of focus. Kids, however, reach their upper limits of focused practice much faster. In general, though, more practice usually means better perfection. A person who practices for a whole hour will attain perfection faster than the one who practices for just around fifteen minutes. The thing to note, however, is that the practice should be mindful, and you should be focused when practicing.

Now, let's look at the quality of how someone practices. For you to get great at something, you need to take into consideration the quality of practice that you undertake. Focused practice will tend to yield much better results.

The main reason for practicing is usually to perfect something. For this to be achieved, you must be mindful of every repetition that you undertake. You must always visualize ahead before any repetition and identify the achievement that you would want to achieve at the end of the practice. Moreover, you must always try to review the achievements made at the end of a repetition. By doing this, you are sure that you will gain better performance at the activity being practiced.

In addition to this continual post and pre-analysis, a focused and effective practice also includes breaking down complex components into small components. For example, when you are learning how to play the piano, you do not just start by jumping into the piano itself. You first have to learn the different keys and master their locations. After breaking down the complex components into simple components, you will later gradually put these small components together and achieve longer sequences.

Mindless Practice

You might have seen an athlete or even a musician engaged in the practice. There is usually a designated pattern that they usually follow. You might have noticed this if you were keen. Some of these distinct patterns include the following:

- **Broken-record method**: In this case, you will only repeat the same thing over and over again. Be it repeating the same key on a piano, the same drills in football, or even the same tennis serve. From a distance, one might view this as practice; however, it is merely just a mindless practice.

- **Autopilot method**: In this case, you will just be on the autopilot system and coast. This means that you will not have a specific goal to achieve at the end of the practice. This is like when you just get to the field and just play aimlessly for the whole time.

- **Hybrid method**: This right here is a combined approach. For example, when you are practicing how to play football, you will play continuously until you reach a point when you do not perform a particular skill right. At this point, you should repeat the skill over and over again until you perfect it.

Three Problems

Mindless practice, however, usually has some setbacks. Here are the three problems that are usually associated with this type of practice:

1. ***It's a waste of time.*** Why is this so? To start with, this practicing method does not really lead to any perfection. This is the reason as to why you might practice for almost a whole day and still not improve all that much at something. In fact, this model of practicing just tends to make you perfect on undesirable habits and errors. This, therefore, increases the likelihood of inconsistent performances. Once these unwanted habits have been attained, you'll find it rigid to let go off these bad behaviors as you move on.

2. ***It makes you less confident.*** Mindless practice makes you less confident. Why is this? They say that you can lie to everyone else, but you cannot lie to yourself. When practicing mindless practice, a part of you will always be aware that you are not practicing in the right way. For this matter, you will always have a sense of uncertainty deep down that just won't go away. This is amid the fact that you are making great progress in what you are doing.

3. ***It's mind-baffling dismal.*** Practicing senselessly is typically like a chore. The measure of achievement, in this situation, is usually signified by the number of times you exercise. This, though, shouldn't be the circumstance. You should've some customary goals that you'd achieve at the conclusion of the training sessions. For instance, when you're practicing on how to play football, you'd set objectives like, "I should be capable of achieving the skill flawlessly by the end of the

4. training session."

How to Accelerate Skill Development

Practicing can be a very complex task to undertake. This is because it requires one to be fully committed and cautious about many things. However, it can be made much easier by just following these five principles:

1. *Focus is everything.* Focused practice tends to yield many more results. Therefore, you should keep your practice sessions as short as possible so as to remain focused. This duration may be as short as ten to twenty minutes and as long as forty-five to sixty minutes.

2. *Timing is everything.* For the practice to be effective, you must choose to do it when you are most active. This can be like in the mornings. Practicing during your most productive times will help you think clearly and stay focused when practicing.

3. *Don't trust your memory.* For any effective practice, you have to carry out an analysis of your progress and goals. What do you want to achieve by the end of the session? What have you achieved at the end of the session? These signs of progress should be noted down on a practice notebook. You

should not try to memorize all your progress. Noting down helps a lot because you will be able to keep track of all activities.

4. *Smarter, not harder.* "Work smart" is a phrase that you are aware of. This phrase also applies during practice. You should always go out of your way and try to come up with simpler ways to achieve perfection in anything that you do. These simple ways will tend to occur naturally when doing an activity because you are the one who has come up with them.

5. *Stay on target with a problem-solving model.* As humans, it is only normal to lose focus when trying to pursue something. It is for this reason that you should keep yourself on task so as to avoid the mindless practice. To help with this, here is a six-step problem-solving model:

Step 1

Define the problem. In this stage, you should ask yourself questions like "What result did I get?" "How would I like the result to sound like?"

Step 2

Analyze the problem. In this stage, you should ask yourself questions like "Where did I go wrong?" "Why does the result occur as it is occurring?"

Step 3

Identify potential solutions. In this stage, you should ask yourself questions like "What can I do to change the result to what you wanted?"

Step 4

Test the potential solutions and select the most effective one. In this stage, you should take into consideration all possible solutions, and choose the best one. This is by asking yourself a question like "Which solution can really yield the best results?"

Step 5

Implement the best solution. At this stage, you should now implement the best solution so as to make the changes permanent.

Step 6

Monitor implementation. After implementing the solution, you should continuously reinforce these solutions so that you can continue producing the result you want.

Maintain your gains at all times

Before we conclude, it is essential to address the reason why you need to maintain your achievements. Achieving the gains is easy but we cannot say the same about maintaining them. It is common to think that once you have acquired what you are looking for, the benefits will stick in you magically and forever. From experience, thinking that way will make you fall back on what you solved sooner than you thought.

Therefore, the question you should ask yourself is this: how do you intend to keep the progress that you have developed so far? How many sessions do you need or how many times do you need to revisit the techniques offered in order to guarantee the longevity of what you have learned?

Have a message that helps you stick to your values, such as 'Use it to live happier and less worried.' Such messages will help you every time you need to troubleshoot future events.

As We Conclude

Practice really does make perfect. This is only achieved through a few contributing factors. These factors can really help one in achieving perfection when followed. Practice, however, should be carried out mindfully. You should be focused and should have a clear mind when practicing. Mindless practicing can lead to perfection in undesired habits and errors rather than perfection in the skills. Therefore, learn to practice mindfully and incorporate it into your daily routine so as to achieve perfection.

Good luck.